KETOGENIC DIET

FOR BEGINNERS

4 Weeks of Fat Burning and
Power Revival
KetogenicDiet for Beginners

MARIA PHILLIPS

CONTENTS

MARIA PHILLIPS

Legal & Disclaimer

The information contained in this book and its contents is not designed to replace or take the place of any form of medical or professional advice; and is not meant to replace the need for independent medical, financial, legal or other professional advice or services, as may be required. The content and information in this book have been provided for educational and entertainment purposes only.

The content and information contained in this book have been compiled from sources deemed reliable, and it is accurate to the best of the Author's knowledge, information, and belief. However, the Author cannot guarantee its accuracy and validity and cannot be held liable for any errors and/or omissions. Further, changes are periodically made to this book as and when needed.

Where appropriate and/or necessary, you must consult a professional (including but not limited to your doctor, attorney, financial advisor or such other professional advisor) before using any of the suggested remedies, techniques, or information in this book.

Upon using the contents and information contained in this book, you agree to hold harmless the Author from and against any damages, costs, and expenses, including any legal fees potentially resulting from the application of any of the information provided by this book. This disclaimer applies to any loss, damages or injury caused by the use and application, whether directly or indirectly, of any advice or information presented, whether for breach of contract, tort, negligence, personal injury, criminal intent, or under any other cause of action.

You agree to accept all risks of using the information presentedinthis book.

You agree that by continuing to read this book, where appropriate and/or necessary, you shall consult a professional (including but not limited to your doctor, attorney, or financial advisor or such other advisor as needed) before using any of the suggested remedies, techniques, or information in this book.

PART 1
KETOGENIC DIET

CHAPTER 1: INTRODUCTION

Hello! I'm Maria Phillips, passionate follower of Ketogenic life style. Keto diet is not a diet; it is a lifestyle. I hate being overweight and having a sufficiently fat body; we should have thin, slimmer, active and energetic body. While following this way of life, you are going to improve your health and beauty with dramatic weight loss. I sincerely recommend you to follow a keto diet and explore benefits yourself.

Previously like top celebrities I espoused plant, vegan, juice and smoothie diet's to gain health, reduce body weight, anti-aging and balances the pH level to avoid serious health problems/diseases like obesity, arthritis and cancer, but however I do exercises and follow the diet still I faced some problems, then after proper research and seeing the results I started to follow a new diet called KETOGENIC DIET, you might hear about it but didn't try it due to more fat intake fear, Actually it is a modified version of Atkins diet.

At first, congratulations for choosing KETOGENIC book for beginners with 4 weeks of fat burning and power revival with sufficient fat, protein, carbs intake, these recipes helps you to lose weight, gain health, energy, and vitality faster. Coming to the facts, there are many other different types of advantages from a keto diet, but due to proper information/guide, people are missing good way to lose weight and eliminating fat from the body to maintain healthy and energetic long life.

There are some ways to make delicious and nutritious keto recipes than just adding bunches of ingredients willy-nilly. So, to avoid this type of recipes, the following chapters will explain clear step of preparation method including health benefits with proper nutritional information chart. Additionally, you will learn different types of helpful tips and tricks to ensure your keto diet habit develops as quickly and smoothly as possible, including how to fully commit to the keto diet without any additional carvings. After that you will find top 35 ultimate keto recipes for rapid health and weight loss in 4 weeks, including perfect meal plan. This recipe will ensure that you will definitely gain energy and lose weight in a short period of time without losing your health.

CHAPTER 2: KETOGENIC DIET AND IT'S LIFESTYLE

The ketogenic eating regimen is anexcessive-fat, low carbohydrate diet that has similar features like Atkins and less-carb diets. Frequently, the energy required for the body is acquired from glucose or sugar, however, while you lessen carbohydrate intake, the body begins burning saved fats for energy. These make your body pass metabolic mode known as catharsis, because of this, hormone insulin could be reduced, automatically release of fatty acids may be greater and whilst fatty acids are transferred to the liver for digestion than it will likely be oxidized and modified to ketones and supplies energy to the mind. Typically, brain cells required glucose as a fuel, but whilst the frame is going to the starvation mode brain gets 25% to 60% of strength from ketones due to low carbohydrate intake and turns protein to glucose for remaining energy, the technique of changing protein too little glucose inside the brain is known as gluconeogenesis.

When you start burning fat cells, routinely body starts decreases weight right away, and you'll feel better inside and also outside. Some of the health benefits that you will achieve while following keto diet are:

Body Weight Lose: The keto diet makes you to reduce weight quicker than different food's as it lowers the insulin level and starts burning stored fats. Due to this process, the body starts to lose weight faster than normal.

Blood Sugar Levels: Blood sugar levels could be advanced as it reduces glucose and glycated hemoglobin within the body and automatically there will be quick improvement in blood sugar levels.

Blood Pressure: Researchers diagnosed that weight reduction plan will result in decrease the blood pressure in obese or overweight people and facilitates to reduce strokes and heart sicknesses.

Cholesterol Levels: Keto helps to lessen the bad cholesterol (Trans fats and saturated fats) and increases good cholesterol (monounsaturated fats and polyunsaturated fats) which are necessary for the body.

Acne: Recent human studies have proven that there is a drastic drop in pimples lesions, pores and skin infection over 10-12 week period of time.

It improves signs and symptoms of epilepsy and different chronic health problems like asthma, arthritis, headache, migraine, inflammation, anemia, heartburn and etc. Keto helps to reverse Alzheimer's signs/symptoms and even kills the cancer cells.

Recently, doctors started to recommend and support a ketogenic eating regimen for neurological issues including autism and mind tumors. Overall, ourketogenic weight loss plan is to force your body into this metabolic state. We don't gain this via starvation of calories; however, we obtain this starvation of carbs. So, in this case you will be overloaded with fats and decrease carbs, this starts to burn ketones as the primary power source to the body.

CHAPTER 3: HISTORY OF KETOGENIC DIET

This type of fasting remedy/treatment followed for curing many diseases by historic Indian and Greek physicians and later in 1911, France conducted and used this fasting approach as a scientist have a look at to cure epilepsy, the eating regimen showed a few outcomes in patient's intellectual capacity development. Dr. Russell Wilder from Maya Clinic named this fasting weight-reduction plan as a "Ketogenic diet" and formally began as a treatment for epilepsy.

In the early 1920s, Drs. Cobb and Lennox at Harvard Medical School started to examine the consequences of starvation, and they had been the first to observe that seizure improvement commonly took place after 2–3 days. Lennox documented that the control of seizures took place thru a change of frame metabolism by using the absence of meals are much less carbohydrate intake in the body forced the body to burn acid-forming fats.

In 1921, Dr. Geyelin became the first person in the American Medical Association convention did a test with fasting as a remedy for epilepsy, and he became the primary to document the cognitive development that could occur with fasting. In 1921, Dr. Wilder on the Mayo Clinic proposed that the benefits of fasting may want to gain if ketonemia produced and he recommended that a ketogenic weight loss program (KD) attempted on epilepsy sufferers. He recommended that the food regimen need to be as powerful as fasting and maintained for a longer duration body. In 1925, Mayo Clinic pronounced that calculation of the Ketogenic Diet for youngsters ought to base on 1 gram of protein consistent with kilogram of body weight, 10–15 grams of carbohydrates in line with the day, and the remainder of the calories in fats. In between 1941 and 1980, Ketogenic Diet has finished prominence inside the textbook on epilepsy in children's.

CHAPTER 4: TYPES OF KETOGENIC DIETS

If your ultimate aim is not to build muscular body, then you may skip this segment. Usually, every muscle builder gets doubt, is carbs are essential to build muscle. The answer is NO; they're now not important for the technique muscle building.

Your glycogen stores can nevertheless be reloaded while on a ketogenic weight loss plan. A ketogenic weight loss plan is one of the notable methods to construct muscle; however, protein consumption performs a vital function here. Especially to benefit body mass, recommended that you need to be taking in approximately 1g to 1.2g protein according to the lean pound of body weight. There are different types of a Ketogenic Diet depending on your requirements.

Standard Ketogenic Diet (SKD): SKD is a classic keto diet known and followed by everyone. It is mainly for a weight loss with high in fats, low in carbs and mild in the protein consumption process is called Standard Ketogenic Diet. In SKD, the maximum intake per day should be 20-50 grams of net carbs.

Targeted Ketogenic Diet (TKD): TKD is modified version of Standard Ketogenic Diet, but consumption of rapid-digesting carbs earlier than exercise (30-60 minutes) with an excessive glycemic index to keep away from stomach disappointed, for nice end result go for glucose primarily based meal plan and attempt to keep away from food items which contain excessive in fructose. Fructose would top off liver glycogen instead of muscle glycogen that is vital to save you on a ketogenic eating regimen. A Targeted Ketogenic Diet gives the platform for keeping exercise overall performance and allows for glycogen re-synthesis without breaking ketosis for prolonged intervals of time. Remember, your publish exercising; food must be low in fat and excessive in protein. If you eat fats after a workout, it is able to reduce muscle recovery and nutrient absorption. So, attempt to avoid eating high-fat meals after exercise.

- 25-50 grams or less of net carbs

- 30-60 mins before sporting activities

- Best for high body activities and athletes

Cyclical Ketogenic Diet (CKD): Cyclical Ketogenic Diet aimed at folks who are doing greater advanced exercising and heavy workouts. For instance, body builders and athletes. Cyclical Ketogenic Diet is to empty muscle glycogen among the carb loads absolutely

- Eating low-carb keto for a few days (50 carbs consistent with day)

- Eating excessive carbs for a few days: this is referred to as the carb-loading state with 450 to 600 grams of carbs consumed in step with the day, this lasts for twenty-four to forty eight hours.

CHAPTER 5: HOW DOES KETOSIS PLAY KEY ROLE IN IMPROVING HEALTH

When you consume more carbohydrates, the body breaks the carbs into glucose to create Adenosine triphosphate; ATP incorporates strength to the location where the energy is wanted, and once gain ATP is divided into Adenosine diphosphate and phosphate, which releases energy relying on reactions. When there is an extra of glucose, it will be transformed into glycogen and stored within the liver and muscle tissues, and further glycogen may be saved as fat, however inside the ketogenic food regimen, the liver begins breaking fats by way of developing fatty acids, and fatty acids damaged into a similar procedure called as ketogenesis. When the body is in the high-fat burning mode, is referred to as ketosis. To enhance and growth this ketone's, our insulin level in bloodstream should be small. Using contemporary's generation, we will degree ketone tiers in the body to serum ketone test. For more weight loss, we ought to have a serum ketones range among 0.5-3mM.

Attain Ketosis:

Achieving ketosis is a pretty easy, however, it looks complex and perplexing with all other statistics to be had right here and the net. Here's the easy trick what you want to do, in step with priority:

Limiting carbohydrates: Mostly, people will keep focus on net carbs, but if you are seeking out the best effects in short time restrict both net carbs and total carbs. Try to stay under 20g net carbs and under the 35g total carbs intake consistent in a day.

Limiting protein: People who come to ketogenic weight loss plan from an Atkins weight loss program forget to restrict their protein. So, you should keep in mind that extra consumption of protein can cause lower your ketosis. Especially, for weight loss, you need to consume among 0.6g and 0.8g protein per pound lean body mass.

Remove fat fear: Fat is he energy source in the ketogenic diet. So, ensure that devour enough fat to your body. Remember, you'll no longer lose weight on keto thru starvation.

Water: You should drink a gallon of water in a day. Mainly to avoid dehydrating, it enables to adjust many critical bodily capabilities and additionally contributes to control your starvation levels.

Avoid snacks: When you have fewer insulin spikes at some stage in the day, it'll tend to weight reduction. Unnecessary snacking may additionally result installs or slow your weight loss goal.

Fasting: Fasting is one of the exceptional ways in reinforce ketone stages continually throughout the day. There are many benefits from intermittent fasting. Such as testosterone,blood lipid and longevity levels.

Exercise/Activities: Everyone knows that exercising and body activities are for a healthy lifestyle. If you need to get best outcomes from your keto diet then including 30 minutes of exercise/activities in a day, even walking can help in losing weight and maintain proper blood sugar levels in the body.

Additional supplements: Even though it isn't necessarily wanted and encouraged, supplementing can assist with a ketogenic weight-reduction plan.

Ways to find that you are in Ketosis:

There are a few shortcuts and hints to attaining most appropriate ketosis. Optimal Ketosis can perfectly finish via dietary nutrition alone. Instant of the usage of some faulty gear, you could discover with easy physical "signs and symptoms" that usually allow you to recognize if you're on the right way or not.

Urination: Keto is a natural diuretic, so in case you are going to the bathroom more regularly than everyday then it is one of the symptoms that you are on right track. These are especially because of elimination of a ketone from body thru urination, lead to more toilet visits for starters.

Mouth dryness: The regular urination leads to dry mouth and will increase thirst. Don't forget to drink required water (gallon) and complement your electrolytes (salt, potassium, magnesium).

Stinky breath: Acetone is a ketone body that partly eliminated via your breath. It can scent sharp like over ripe fruit (similar to nail polish remover). It's only transient for starters and goes away in long term process.

Energized and hunger less: Normally, after passing "keto flu," you'll revel in and experience lower in starvation degree, and this level is known as energized mental level.

Ketosis Testers:

There are many home kits that help to discover and find out ketones levels in your body. Some of ketones level finder is:

Breathalyzer: These are one of the most inexpensive methods to find ketone concentrations inside the body. Normally, whilst you are on the ketogenic food regimen, your breath can have a wonderful scent; this is especially due to acetones.

Ketone strips: Urine ketone strips are one of the different cheap and smooth methods to find an extra of ketone bodies may be excreted from the body in urine, but this isn't so powerful.

Ketone meter: The blood ketone meter is one of the high-quality and effective techniques to find ketone stages inside the body, it's little high priced, however you could display your ketone ranges on a daily basis for the entire weight reduction in much less length.

Self-realization: You can feel from your body, for example: by using your distinguishable breath, alternate in urine color and fruity sweat scent. If you find these changes in you, then you are definitely in ketosis.

Basic Tips and Tricks:

Before you start every day, take into account and remind yourself about outstanding advantages you acquire whilst following a ketogenic eating regimen and tell yourself that you may do that for weight loss and gain energy with proper health.

First step: Begin every day with a few glasses of water, including a cup of detox tea with herbal sweetener, so that it will offer cleansing guide on your kidneys and liver for better and efficient results.

Monitor: Don't neglect to take measurements and photos earlier than you start your food regimen that is the quality way to screen your development and keep in mind this is not just for weight loss but for a healthier lifestyle.

Reward: When you achieved weekly level, praise yourself with an additional smoothie and remind yourself about extraordinary advantages that you are gained and going to obtain in your life.

Prepared ingredients: Depending to your next day

plan, you could prepare required ingredients earlier to keep away from confusions and additionally you may make a best liked recipe based to your desire.

Measuring kit: It is vital to have size package to test your daily ketone levels, this helps you find and also keep track on your progress weather you are in the right course and meal plan to reduce weight in a short period of time.

Basic Mistakes:

More protein: In a ketogenic food plan, we need to apprehend eating more protein will lead to gluconeogenesis, which converts the amino acids to glucose and leads to glucose levels in the body. Just don't forget, you ought to increase your fat intake.

More nuts: Nuts are filled with a lot of fat and also don't forget they have stuffed with lots of calories. So, try and eat nuts in minimum quantity or replace nuts with high-fat fruits like Avocado, Durian, Akee and Coconut.

Less fat: Don't forget, fat intake need to be more than protein and carbs intake. People's consumption of fat is nearly equal to protein, but it is inaccurate, the ratio of intake needs to be 75% fat, 20% protein and 5% carbs.

Repeating same meal: When you are preparing the same kind of meal every day, you'll be bored and lose interest to follow diet. So, to keep your spirit high, make different variety of recipes with fewer carbs.

Basic Exercises:

For any diet, necessarytraining plays a key role to start a new habit, for example, 15 minutes of body movements per day will help a lot in a daily life. Let's see some of the important and necessarychanges that help to lose weight faster when you follow a proper diet.

Park then walk: I think you already heard about this technique, but I am 100% sure that this works. Instead of parking in front of your office or workplace, park little far for next parking lot, which makes you walk and helps you to proper blood flow in your body.

Prefer staircase: Instead of using the elevator in an office or any other place, use staircase which squeezes your muscles of the body and keeps you away from joints, ligaments, and bone pains. Doing like this will burn more calories.

Shopping: If you don't have a big shopping list, then this is the right time to use your body. Keep the bags over your shoulders and walk for selecting items and carrying the heavy grocery items with your hands is a great workout and the same time you will be finishing you're shopping for whole weeks also.

Stretch yourself: Sitting in front of your desk or computer is extremely hard for the body, but there are lots ways that you can work while sitting. One the best way is toned your legs at regular intervals and whenever you go to the toilet or coffee, stretch your whole body and go. Upgrade to the stability ball instead of sitting in a regular chair.

Self-preparation: Do you know that cooking food by yourself for breakfast, lunch, and dinner is also an exercise which helps your body and tries to use more calories and avoid future health problems?

PART 2
KETOGENIC
MACRONUTRIENTS
AND FOOD DETAILS

CHAPTER 6: BRIEF OVERVIEW OF THE KETOGENIC FOOD ITEMS

Remember yourself that ketogenic is excessive in fat, moderate in protein, and really low in carbohydrates. Your nutrient consumption should be something around seventy five% fats, 20% protein, and five% carbohydrate.

Mostly in between 20-30g of internet carbs is suggested for normal weight-reduction plan however for higher result try and the lower your carbohydrate intake and glucose levels. If you're following the ketogenic eating regimen for weight loss, it's a very good idea to preserve the track of both your total carbs and net carbs consumption for each day.

Protein need to constantly devour as wished with fats by calculating energy consumption in line with day. You might be questioning, "What's a net carb?" It's simple! The internet carbs are your overall nutritional carbohydrates, minus the entire fiber. I absolutely propose you to keep overall carbs below 35g and net carbs beneath 25g.

If you're feeling famished within the path of the day, you may have snacks like nuts, seeds, cheeses, or peanut butter to control your appetite (this will have an impact in your healthful weight-reduction plan weight loss plan).

Following a ketogenic weight loss plan isn't the very best problem to deal with, especially whilst you don't recognize what you need to devour. Let us see a few vital ketogenic food plan food, listing to get an idea to make scrumptious meals recipes without becoming bored.

Fats and Oil

When you are on the ketogenic diet, fat will play a sizeable position on your daily calorie intake. Fats are vital to our bodies, so ensure that you devour right sort of fat to keep away from incorrect main. The Important Fats that plays a key position in a Ketogenic Diet are:

Saturated fats: These fats are very important to keep your immune machine wholesome, scientific studies says that they have no association with risk of coronary heart disorder and enhance HDL/LDL cholesterol levels.

Polyunsaturated fat: These are normally to be had in the form of vegetable oils and processed polyunsaturated fats are horrific for the body, for you to worsen HDL/LDL levels of cholesterol and natural polyunsaturated fats are suitable for the frame to enhance HDL/LDL cholesterol levels.

Monounsaturated fats: These fats are widely known

and used for a healthful lifestyle. These improve the insulin resistance and higher HDL/LDL cholesterol levels. Olive and sunflower oil are substantial examples of healthy monounsaturated fats.

Some of the ketogenic food regimen ingredients which can be a brilliant supply of fat and oils are (typically select natural and grass-fed resources)

Protein

Your best supply in relation to protein is choosing something grass fed or organic and the use of eggs. This will allow reducing your bacteria and steroid hormone intake.

Fish: Mostly try and eat anything this is caught wild like salmon, mackerel, catfish, tuna, mahi-mahi, flounder, cod, halibut, snapper, and trout

Shellfish: Crab, mussels, oysters, lobster, clams, squid and scallops

Whole eggs: If feasible, try and get loose-variety/natural eggs from the nearby marketplace. You can put together them in specific approaches and patterns like boiled, poached, fried, scrambled and deviled

Poultry: Chicken, Duck, Quail, Pheasant. If viable, satisfactory option can be free variety or natural

Meat: Beef, Veal, Goat, Lamb, and special wild recreation. Grass fed is preferred because it has a better fatty acid rely

Pork: Pork chops, red meat loin, and ham (check for sugar levels)

Bacon/Sausage: Before purchasing test exactly the labels for something cured in sugar, or if it has extra fillers

Peanut butter: Get pure and herbal peanut butter; however, be cautious as they have got excessive counts of carbohydrates and Omega-6s. If you want, you can transfer to macadamia nut butter

Vegetables

While on a ketogenic weight-reduction plan, try to get greens that develop above the ground and sparkling leafy greens (nice choice is natural) however if you may get them don't worry. Research display that the organic and the non-organic veggies have the identical dietary values and characteristicsAlways attempt to keep away from starchy greens like Peas, Corn, Potatoes, Parsnips, amps, Beans and Legumes

Seeds/Nuts

Roasted seeds and nuts and seeds are satisfactory to cast off any anti-vitamins. If possible, broadly speaking keep away from peanuts; truly, they may come underneath legumes, not advocated in the ketogenic diet food listing.

- Almonds, walnuts, and macadamias are the best regarding your carbs count, and you could consume in small amounts to lower carbs intake

- Pistachios and cashews are better in carbs, so make which you count number them cautiously while ingesting

- Nuts are high in Omega-6 Fatty Acids, so keep away from over consumption

27

- Seed and nut flours are the exceptional substitute for regular flour, consisting of almond flour and milled flaxseed

Beverages

The ketogenic food plan has an herbal diuretic impact, so dehydration is common in the planning stage of diet for most people. If you're vulnerable to urinary tract infections or bladder ache, you need to be especially organized for it. Usually, we are alleged to drink 8 glasses of water in keeping with the day? It performs a great role in our frame, and it's critical and especially recommended to maintain hydrated. Drink drinks day and night time, drink it like normal paintings.

- Drink masses of water

- Coffee

- Tea (endorsed Herbal)

Sweeteners

Staying away from candy items is the first-rate wager. It will assist manage your cravings to a minimal level, which mainly contributes to accomplishing fulfillment on the ketogenic weight loss program. If you like to have a candy first-class preference is an artificial sweetener. Try to move for liquid sweeteners, together with Erythritol, Liquid stevia, Liquid Sucralose and Xylitol.

CHAPTER7: STEP BY STEP GUIDELINES TO START KETOGENIC DIET

Part 1: Starting a Ketogenic Diet

Step 1. Talk to your health practitioner and get thought of him

Step 2. Recognize and become aware of possible risks of a ketogenic weight-reduction plan

Step 3. Start with an ordinary low-carb weight loss program to ease yourself into nutritional ketosis

Step 4. Calculate every day your macronutrient consumption

Part 2: Modify your Ketogenic Diet Based on your Requirements

Step 5. Eat daily most effective 20 or 30 grams of carbs

Step 6. Eat minimal 2–8 ounce of protein several instances an a day

Step 7. Eat extra fat with all of your meal to balance

Step 8. Don't assume and pressure too much regarding your calorie intake/consumption

Step 9. Try to drink more water and be more hydrated

Part 3: Losing Weight on your Diet Process

Step 10. Check whether you are in ketosis or not via the use of a keto meter and different keto analyzers

Step 11. Check and look for ketosis symptoms (keto flu)

Step 12. Identify that your health has stepped forward or now not (after two weeks)

PART 3
KETOGENICMEAL
PLANAND RECIPES

CHAPTER 8: A KETOGENIC 4 WEEKS MEAL PLAN

WEEK 1

Our primary motive is very simple inside the first week. At the primary week, you don't need to do hard transition because it is very difficult clearly to take away your meals cravings. We are going to don't forget leftovers matters, due to the fact why to prepare dinner same meals again and again? Breakfast is some thing I normally cook with leftover items, wherein I don't have to fear for morning and no need to assume and experience pressures approximately it.

The first symptoms which you are stepping into ketosis are referred to as the "keto flu" wherein headaches, fatigue, brain fogginess, and so forth can disturb your frame. Make positive and bear in mind to ingesting plenty of water with salt (I endorse a gallon in keeping with day). The ketogenic healthy diet weight-reduction plan is a natural diuretic, and you'll be peeing greater than ordinary. Take below consideration that you're peeing out electrolytes, and you could wager that you'll be having an considerable headache no time. Make effective that your salt intake and water consumption immoderate enough than regular, to allow your body to re-hydrate and re-deliver your electrolytes.

Breakfast

For breakfast, you need to do a little thing that may be brief, easy, tasty, and leftovers. I suggest beginning day 1 want to be on the weekend. This way, you could make something with a view to very last you for the whole week. The first week is all approximately simplicity.

Lunch

Lunch goes to be easy. Normally, it'll be salad and meat, spread in excessive-fat dressings. If you aren't feeling like making, you can use leftover meat from preceding nights or use smooth available canned chook/fish. If you do use canned meats, make sure that you examine seemingly the label for hidden carbs. Additionally, you could also add spices and seasonings in your salad for your liking. Just be careful approximately garlic and onion powder, however extraordinary spices can have negligible carbs.

Dinner

Dinner is going to be a mixture of leafy vegetables (by and massive broccoli and spinach) with a few meat. Remember, we are going to immoderate fats and mild protein consumption.

Note: No dessert for the first 2 weeks and keep in mind to drink lots of water with little salt.

Shopping List:

All time basic shopping list: Ghee, Salt, Baking soda, Allspice, Herbs, Chili, Garlic, Ginger, Sauces (soy, tomato, marinara), Article sugars (stevia, ethanol), Nuts (all types), Sesame, poppy seeds (toasted), Lemon (juice and zest), Pepper, Coconut milk, Vinegars, Fruit extracts, Butter, Maple syrup.

Breakfast shopping list: Eggs 10, Almond flour 1 packet, Chia flour 1 packet, Gobi berries 1 oz, Ackee 2.5 oz, Mascarpone cheese 2 oz, Ricotta cheese 3.5 oz, Cream 2 oz, Coconut flour 1 packet, Yogurt 1packet, Mozzarella 4 oz, Tuna 1oz, Onions 3, Cauliflower 1

Lunch shopping list: Flax meal 1 packet, Eggs 6, Sausage 2 oz, Cream 1 oz, Halloumi cheese 2 slices, Kimchi 2 oz, Mascarpone cheese 6 oz, Vegetable mix 1 packet, Tomatoes 7, Salmon 1 lb, Asparagus small packet, Rind 4 oz, Wrappers (rolls) 8, Bacon 2 oz, Mushrooms 1packet, Cabbage 1, Parmesan cheese 1 oz, Mozzarella 1 oz

Snack shopping list: Pumpkin 1, Nuts 1 packet, Almond flour 1 packet, Chia flour 1 packet, Flax flour 1 packet

Dinner shopping list: Pork 1 lb, Kumatoes 2 lb, Onions 2, Mozzarella 15 oz, Mascarpone cheese 8 oz, Prawns 3 oz, Broccoli 2 oz, Squash 35 oz, Tuna 1 lb, Halloumi cheese 2 slices, Spinach 1 oz

Day	BREAKFAST	LUNCH	SNACK	DINNER
Day 1	Orange Bread	Cheese Cabbage Sausage	Energy Peanut Bars	Winter Cheese Sandwich
Day 2	Mascarpone Ackee	Sesame Layered Turkey Chicken	-	Coconut Pork Stew
Day 3	Yogurt Olive Pancake	Winter Vegetable Stew	-	Cheesy KumatoSandwich
Day 4	Tunaroni Pizza	Grilled Mascarpone Salmon	Durian Mug Cake	-
Day 5	Chia Pancakes	Wild Bacon Mushroom	-	Forest Mushroom Broccoli Bowl
Day 6	Mascarpone Ackee	Bacon Pepper Omelet	Protein Flax Bars	-
Day 7	Yogurt Olive Pancake	AlmondKimchi Bowl	-	Roasted Walnut Tuna Filet

WEEK 2

Wow, already week 1 is over. I hope you're nonetheless doing nicely on a weight-reduction plan and feature located an easy manner to maintain track. Again this week, we're going to keep easy breakfast. We're going to introduce keto coffee. It's a mixture of coconut oil, butter, and heavy cream in your coffee. When you mix the oil, butter, and cream together, it simply provides an effete richness on your espresso that I am quite confident that you'll adore it.

Breakfast

For breakfast, we are going to exchange a touch bit and going to introduce Keaton coffee. I recognize some humans received find it irresistible. If you don't like coffee, then sieve the tea.

Why keto espresso?

Fat loss: Clean and simple, the consumption of medium-chain triglycerides (MCT) has been proven to cause greater losses in fat tissue (adipose tissue), in both animals and humans.

Fat consumption leads to significant quantities of electricity, efficient utilization of electricity, and more efficient manner to weight loss faster than an everyday weight-reduction plan (it's the primary element of this food plan).

Energy extension: Research has proven that the fast fee of oxidation in Medium Chain Fatty Acids (MCFAs) leads to a growth in power. Mainly, MCFAs are transformed into ketones, are absorbed in a different way inside the frame compared to everyday oils, and produces more power. Feel loose to feature sweetener and spices (cinnamon, stevia, vanilla extract) to this in case you're no longer the most important fan of the candy flavor.

Lunch

We're going to keep simple and assimilate more meat (you could use left out). Green veggies fry or soups and excessive-fat dressings are critical gadgets. Keep a list of fats and protein intake due to the fact taking right amount is crucial.

Dinner

Dinner is pretty simple. Meats, greens, high-fat dressings are vital for keto. Don't ever assume much approximately weight reduction within the first 2 weeks; straightforward and steady allows reaching success.

Shopping List:

All time basic shopping list: Ghee, Salt, Baking soda, Allspice, Herbs, Chili, Garlic, Ginger, Sauces (soy, tomato, marinara), Article sugars (stevia, ethanol), Nuts (all types), Sesame, poppy seeds (toasted), Lemon (juice and zest), Pepper, Coconut milk, Vinegars, Fruit extracts, Butter, Maple syrup.

Breakfast shopping list: Eggs 8, Almond flour 1 packet, Chia flour 1 packet, Cream cheese 11 oz., Mozzarella 4 oz., Bacon 6 slices, Cabbage 1, Cheddar cheese 3 oz.

Lunch shopping list: All nuts 1 packet, Duck 14 oz., Bacon 4 oz., Lettuce 1, Mascarpone cheese 7 oz., Anchovies 1, Spinach 4 oz., Rapini 1, Collard 1 Parmesan cheese 1 oz., Eggs 4

Avocado 2, Asparagus 2 oz., Carrot 1, Crab 4 oz., Tomatoes 5, Turkey 1 oz., Chicken breast 2 oz., Gobi berries 5, Goat cheese 5 oz., Rind 1 oz., Squash 3 oz., Mozzarella 6 oz.

Snack shopping list: Cream, Coconut milk, Raspberries 2 oz., Cocoa powder, Almond milk 1 packet, Egg 1

Dinner shopping list: Eggs 15, Mascarpone cheese 2 oz., Mozzarella 7 oz., Avocado 2, Parmesan cheese 2 oz., Tuna 4 oz., Onions 3 oz., Turkey 1 lb, Black bean 2 oz., Lamb 2 oz., Better melon 1, Bacon 6 oz., Cheddar cheese 3.5 oz., Squash 1

Day	BREAKFAST	LUNCH	SNACK	DINNER
Day 8	Fatty Bagels	Sweet Cheese Duck Salad	Coco-Cream Smoothie	Mascarpone Salmon Wraps
Day 9	Purple Casserole	Chicken Dill Salad	-	-
Day 10	Maple Chia Waffles	Green Nut Salad	Raspberry Cheese Smoothie	Tuna Omelet
Day 11	Yummy Filled Eggs	Crab Carrot Salad	-	Bacon Cheese Layer
Day 12	Yummy Chia Pancakes	Boiled Avocado Salad	Almond HorchataSmoothie	-
Day 13	Maple Chia Waffles	Goji Salad	-	Summer Bacon Fry
Day 14	Purple Casserole	Turkey Salad	Raspberry Cheese Smoothie	-

WEEK 3

This week we're going too speedy and going to consume fat within the morning itself and rapid until time for supper. I endorse keeping minimum 12 hours hole among morning breakfast and dinner offers higher and quicker consequences. For instance: Have breakfast at 7 am after which dinner at 7 pm. By doing like this, the frame is going to fasting state, due to this kingdom body will spoil down greater fats and stored for the strength. There are some advantages of intermittent fasting. Some of them are blood lipid levels, longevity, and needed intellectual lucidity. If you experience it is exclusive to do a fast, then no trouble. Go returned to week 1 and collect revel in.

Breakfast

We're going to extra fats in breakfast like a closing week. This time we are going to double the quantity of keto espresso (or tea) by way of increasing the quantity of coconut oil, butter, and heavy cream (really tries and preserves us full until supper time). Don't forget about to drink water positive that you're staying hydrated.

Lunch

Here comes FASTING, don't worry the morning fats will keep you enjoy energized. Make sure you drink masses of water consistent with day and 1 smoothie, on the way to make you to come out of food carving.

Dinner

Dinner is going to be easy with soup or stews. Meats, greens, and fats are nearly usually going to be the dinner quota. Don't fear, this week we are going to devour dessert items.

Shopping List:

All time basic shopping list: Ghee, Salt, Baking soda, Allspice, Herbs, Chili, Garlic, Ginger, Sauces (soy, tomato, marinara), Article sugars (stevia, ethanol), Nuts (all types), Sesame, poppy seeds (toasted), Lemon (juice and zest), Pepper, Coconut milk, Vinegars, Fruit extracts, Butter, Maple syrup.

Breakfast shopping list: Eggs 10, Almond flour 1 packet, Chia flour 1 packet, Goji berries 1 oz., Ackee 2.5 oz., Mascarpone cheese 2 oz., Ricotta cheese 3.5 oz., Cream 2 oz., Coconut flour 1 packet, Yogurt 1packet, Mozzarella 4 oz., Tuna 1oz, Onions 3, Cauliflower 1

Lunch shopping list: Flax meal 1 packet, Eggs 6, Sausage 2 oz., Cream 1 oz., Halloumi cheese 2 slices, Kimchi 2 oz., Mascarpone cheese 6 oz., Vegetable mix 1 packet, Tomatoes 7, Salmon 1 lb, Asparagus small packet, Rind 4 oz., Wrappers (rolls) 8, Bacon 2 oz., Mushrooms 1packet, Cabbage 1, Parmesan cheese 1 oz., Mozzarella 1 oz.

Snack shopping list: Almond flour 1 packet, Cabbage 1.5 oz., Cheddar cheese 5 oz., Mascarpone cheese 4 oz., Eggs 4, Cream 10 oz., Chocolates 2, Chia flour 1 packet, Cocoa powder 2 oz.

Dinner shopping list: Pork 1 lb, Kumatoes 2 lb, Onions 2, Mozzarella 15 oz., Mascarpone cheese 8 oz., Prawns 3 oz., Broccoli 2 oz., Squash 35 oz., Tuna 1 lb, Halloumi cheese 2 slices, Spinach 1 oz.

Day	BREAKFAST	LUNCH	SNACK	DINNER
Day 15	Tunaroni Pizza	Rind Squash Rolls	Cabbage Biscuits	Winter Cheese Sandwich
Day 16	Chia Pancakes	Sesame Layered Turkey Chicken	Crunchy Chia Biscuits	Winter Cheese Sandwich
Day 17	Orange Bread	-	-	-
Day 18	Yogurt Olive Pancake	Grilled Mascarpone Salmon	-	Roasted Walnut Tuna Filet
Day 19	Mascarpone Ackee	-	-	Coconut Pork Stew
Day 20	Orange Bread	Wild Bacon Mushroom	Banana Bombs	-
Day 21	Tunaroni Pizza	Bacon Pepper Omelet	-	Forest Mushroom Broccoli Bowl

WEEK 4

This week we're going observe strict intermittent fasting. So, we're going to keep away from breakfast and lunch. Remember, this week your pleasant buddy will be Water! If you can't stay with none meals, then drink coffee, tea, flavored water because liquids make you forget about stomach growling. Don't worry your body will mechanically modify with time. It's impossible to do fasting comply with week 2 once more. Remember, there are outstanding fitness benefits and improves your self-discipline to do notable matters.

Breakfast

This week we're fasting! Black coffee and tea are going to be your best pal, if you are not preferred of black espresso, then pass for green tea, it has a whole lot of fitness benefits. Some of the benefits of green tea are:

Polyphenols: These act as antioxidants to your body. One of the maximum powerful antioxidant in inexperienced tea is Epigallocatechingallate (EGCG), which has proven to be powerfully in the direction of fatigue.

Active mind characteristic: Not most effective inexperienced tea consists of caffeine; however, it additionally has Ltheanine, which is an amino acid. L-Ltheanine will grow your GABA hobby, which improves tension, dopamine, and alpha waves.

Increased metabolic rate: Research results suggest that green tea can enhance your metabolic rate. In combination with the caffeine, this lets in to expand 15% fat oxidization.

Lunch

Lunch should be plenty of water and smoothies. When you're skipping your breakfast and lunch, you ought to hold yourself very hydrated. Don't overlook to drink minimal four liters of water in step with day and 2 to 3 smoothies.

Dinner

Dinner goes to be a competition for you; it includes lots of meals with dessert to cover the bases! In this week's meal time will be your favorite time. I suggest before everything destroys your speed with a small snack, then after 30-45 minutes devour. Usually, you need 2 meals to get to macros.

Shopping List:

All time basic shopping list: Ghee, Salt, Baking soda, Allspice, Herbs, Chili, Garlic, Ginger, Sauces (soy, tomato, marinara), Article sugars (stevia, ethanol), Nuts (all types), Sesame, poppy seeds (toasted), Lemon (juice and zest), Pepper, Coconut milk, Vinegars, Fruit extracts, Butter, Maple syrup.

Breakfast shopping list: Eggs 8, Almond flour 1 packet, Chia flour 1 packet, Cream cheese 11 oz., Mozzarella 4 oz., Bacon 6 slices, Cabbage 1, Cheddar cheese 3 oz.

Lunch shopping list: Broth 5 cups, Bacon 2 oz., Broccoli 1, Mascarpone cheese 3 oz., Lamb 2 lb, Cream cheese 21 oz., Sausage 7, Tomatoes 10, Red chard 10, Eggs 8, Turkey 2 lb

Snack shopping list: Pumpkin 1, Almond milk 1 packet, Cream, Butter

Dinner shopping list: Eggs 15, Mascarpone cheese 2 oz., Mozzarella 7 oz., Avocado 2, Parmesan cheese 2 oz., Tuna 4 oz., Onions 3 oz., Turkey 1 lb, Black bean 2 oz., Lamb 2 oz., Better melon 1, Bacon 6 oz., Cheddar cheese 3.5 oz., Squash 1

Day	BREAKFAST	LUNCH	SNACK	DINNER
Day 22	Yummy Chia Pancakes	Turkey Ghee Soup	Pumpkin Smoothie	Vinaigrette Lamb Fry
Day 23	Yummy Filled Eggs	Mixed Squash Salad	-	-
Day 24	Maple Chia Waffles	Red ChardCheese Soup	-	Coconut Turkey Stew
Day 25	Purple Casserole	-	Vanilla Cream Smoothie	-
Day 26	-	Lamb Sausage Soup	-	Summer Bacon Fry
Day 27	Fatty Bagels	Bacon Broccoli Soup	-	Tuna Omelet
Day 28	Yummy Filled Eggs	-	Vanilla Cream Smoothie	Vanilla Cream Smoothie

CHAPTER 9: KETOGENIC RECIPES

KetoSeasoned Coffee

Ingredients
- Coffee 240ml
- Unsalted butter 1 tbsp.
- Coconut oil 1 tbsp.
- Heavy cream 1 tbsp.
- Seasonings to taste

Preparation Method
1. At first, make 1 cup of coffee and put in serving glass
2. Now, add the butter, after it ooze, then coconut oil, heavy cream and mix well
3. It gives creaminess and extra flavor to the coffee
4. If desired, add your favorite seasonings like cinnamon, nutmeg, or allspice with a splash of liquid stevia
5. Mix it all together very well using a hand blender and enjoy the taste

Nutritional Information
- Preparation Time: 5 minutes
- Serving per Recipe: 1
- Calories: 273
- Protein: 0g
- Fat: 30g
- Carbohydrates: 1g

KETOGENICBREAKFAST RECIPES

RECIPE 1: ORANGE BREAD

Ingredients
Bread

- Stevia 2 tbsp.
- Ghee 2 tbsp.
- Egg 1
- Egg yolk 2
- Orange juice 2 tsp.
- Vanilla extracts 1 tsp.
- Almond flour 0.5 oz.
- Baking powder ½ tsp.
- Chia flour 2 tsp.
- Pinch of salt

Goji Berry Glaze

- Butter 2 tbsp.
- Goji berry 1 oz.
- Erythritol3 tbsp.

Preparation Method

1. At first, preheat the oven to 350F. In a mixing bowl, add all bread ingredients together and mix well until it forms a nice batter.
2. Line a baking sheet with parchment paper and put batter (if desired, you can create your own bread shape).
3. Place in a preheated oven and bake for 10 minutes and let it cool for 5 minutes.
4. Meanwhile, prepare glaze by adding all ingredients in a small bowl and mix using hand mixer.
5. Put this glaze in the fridge for minimum 30 minutes, using a spoon, gently glaze your bread and enjoy the taste.

Nutritional Information

- Preparation Time: 15 minutes
- Total servings: 2
- Calories: 189 (per serving)
- Fat: 17.1g
- Protein: 7.9g
- Carbs: 2.4g

RECIPE 2: MASCARPONE ACKEE

Ingredients

- Eggs yolk 2
- Eggs white 3
- Almond flour 2 tbsp.
- Ricotta cheese 3.5 oz.
- Mascarpone cheese 1 oz.
- Vanillas extract ½ tsp.
- Ghee 1 tbsp.
- Cream of tartar ½ tsp.
- Baking soda ¼ tsp.
- Ackee 2.5 oz.
- Stevia 10 drops

Preparation Method

1. At first, preheat your oven to 350F. In a separate bowl add egg yolks, vanilla extract, ricotta cheese, mascarpone and stevia.
2. Other side beat egg whites with baking soda and cream of tartar until they become thick and form soft peaks.
3. Now add egg whites mixture to egg yolk mixture and very gently fold in and slowly add the almond flour.
4. Place the sliced akee onto a baking dish lined with parchment paper and greased with ghee.
5. Top with the pancake mixture and add more akee on top. Spray with ghee and place in preheated oven. Set timer to 15 minutes until slightly browned and serve warm.

Nutritional Information

- Preparation Time: 25 minutes
- Total servings: 2
- Calories: 353 (per serving)
- Fat: 26.9g
- Protein: 14.6g
- Carbs: 5.8g

RECIPE 3: YOGURT OLIVE PANCAKE

Ingredients

Pancakes

- Large eggs 2
- Coconut flour 1 tbsp.
- Coconut flakes 1 tbsp.
- Almond flour 1 tbsp.
- Baking soda ¼ tsp.
- Coconut milk 3 tbsp.
- Cinnamon powder ½ tsp.
- Ghee 1 tbsp.
- Stevia 10 drops

Topping

- Yogurt 4.5 oz.
- Cinnamon ½ tsp.
- Fresh olives 4
- Blackberry syrup 2 tbsp.

Preparation Method

1. At first, whisk the egg in a bowl using fork and mix coconut flour, coconut flakes, almond flour, cinnamon, baking soda, stevia and coconut milk.
2. In another bowl, mix the yogurt with cinnamon and keep aside. Now, prepare your pan by applying ghee and add 2 tablespoon of the batter on the pan. Cook for 10 minutes each side.
3. When you finished all pancakes, place on a serving plate by creating two layers of pancakes and yogurt. Top each of them with freshly chopped olives, sprinkle with cinnamon and enjoy the taste.

Nutritional Information

- Preparation Time: 20 minutes
- Total servings: 8
- Calories: 588 (per serving)
- Fat: 45.5g
- Protein: 29.5g
- Carbs: 12.1g

RECIPE 4: TUNARONI PIZZA

Ingredients

- Shredded mozzarella 2.5 oz.
- Shredded mascarpone 1 oz.
- Marinara sauce 4 oz.
- Pepperoni 4 slices
- Tuna 1 oz.
- Basil ½ tsp.
- Onions slices 2 tbsp.
- Parsley 1 tbsp.
- Oregano ½ tsp.
- Ghee 1 tbsp.

Preparation Method

1. At first, put frying pan over medium heat and add mozzarella cheese, mascarpone cheese (keep little both cheese for topping) and cook for 5 minutes or until cheese is caramelized.

2. Don't forget to use a spatula to avoid sticking it to the pan. Now, pour marinara sauce over top and spread it all over cheese.

3. Sprinkle the remaining cheese's over top of that and add slices of pepperoni, tuna and onions.

4. Season with herbs (basil, oregano) and wait until the top layer of cheese has melted, let it cool for 2 minutes and before serving add ghee then enjoy the taste.

Nutritional Information

- Preparation Time: 12 minutes
- Total servings: 1
- Calories: 544 (per serving)
- Fat: 42.9g
- Protein: 17.4g
- Carbs: 7.4g

RECIPE 5: CHIA PANCAKES

Ingredients

- Chia meal 1 cup
- Large eggs 2
- Maple syrup 1 tbsp.
- Cauliflowers paste/puree 2 fl oz.
- Cream ¼ cup
- Ghee2 tbsp.
- All spice 1 tsp.
- Baking soda½ tsp.
- Salt to taste

Preparation Method

1. Mix eggs, cauliflowerpaste/puree, maple, cream and ghee together without lumps.
2. Mix chia meal, all spice, baking soda and salt together in separate bowl.
3. Slowly start adding wet mixture (step1) to get smooth consistency by adding butter.
4. Heat the pan and grease the pan with butter, then add the pancake batter into the pan and cook until bubbles appears on the top.
5. Flip it and cook other side until browned and serve when it is warm for a nice taste.

Nutritional Information

- Preparation Time: 15 minutes
- Total servings: 8
- Calories: 199.5 (per serving)
- Fat: 16.6g
- Protein: 8.1g
- Carbs: 4g

RECIPE 6: FATTY BAGELS

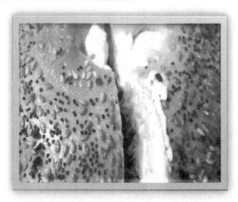

Ingredients

Bagels

- Almond flour 2 oz.
- Large egg 1
- Grated mozzarella 4 oz.
- Cream cheese 2 tbsp.
- Salt to taste

Toppings

- Ghee 1 tbsp.
- Sesame seeds 1 tsp.
- Poppy seeds 1 tsp.

Fillings

- Garlic pesto 2 tbsp.
- Cream cheese 2 tbsp.
- Herb leaves 1 cup
- Pepper 3 tsp.
- Bacon slices 6 (grilled)

Preparation Method

1. At first, preheat your oven to 390F. In a small bowl, mix almond flour, egg, salt and make dough balls then keep aside for 10 minutes.
2. Meantime, melt cream cheese, mozzarella and pour on dough and mix well. Now, slowly split the dough into 3 pieces and try to roll into round shaped logs (like donuts).
3. Now, brush the ghee over it and sprinkle sesame seeds over it and bake in preheated oven for 20 minutes or until it turns to golden color.
4. When bagels are finished, place cream cheese, pesto then adds bacon, herb leaves, pepper on top of bagels and enjoy the taste.

Nutritional Information

- Preparation Time: 35 minutes
- Total servings: 3
- Calories: 615.3 (per serving)
- Fat: 54g
- Protein: 30g
- Carbs: 6g

RECIPE 7: YUMMY FILLED EGGS

Ingredients

- Large eggs 6 (boiled)
- Light soy sauce 120ml
- Water 240ml
- Vinegar 30ml
- Garlic powder 1 tsp.
- Cream cheese 4 oz.
- Thyme 1 tbsp.
- Chili powder 1 tsp.
- Coriander powder ¼ tsp.
- Ghee 2 tbsp.
- Chili powder 1 tsp. (topping)
- Salt and black pepper to taste

Preparation Method

1. At first, mix water, soy sauce, vinegar, garlic powder in a small bowl and keep aside.
2. Soak the eggs in sauce and refrigerate for 2 hours then cut into half and egg yolks separately.
3. Now mix egg yolk, cream, thyme, salt and pepper in a mixing bowl then stuff into egg white.
4. Finally, sprinkle chili powder, coriander powder over it then add ghee over every piece and enjoy the delicious taste.

Nutritional Information

- Preparation Time: 15 minutes
- Total servings: 4
- Calories: 236 (per serving)
- Fat: 24.1g
- Protein: 12.2g
- Carbs: 3.3g

RECIPE 8: PURPLE CASSEROLE

Ingredients

Puree

- Purple cabbage 1
- Heavy cream 2 tbsp.
- Ghee 1 tbsp.
- Shredded cheddar cheese 1 oz.
- Ginger ½ tbsp.
- Garlic powder 1 tsp.
- Salt and pepper to taste

Layer

- Cream cheese 6 oz.
- Shredded cheddar cheese 2 oz.
- Salsa 1 oz.

Topping

- Shredded parmashen cheese 2.5 oz.
- Basil 2 tbsp.

Preparation Method

1. Make puree, blend the cabbage, cheese, and ginger, garlic, and salt, pepper using a blender and put in a bowl. Add cream, ghee, and place in microwave oven for 10 minutes on high and keep aside.
2. Now, make layer by placing cream cheese, shredded cheese, salsa in a microwave safe bowl for 30 seconds until cheese soften.
3. In a large bowl make casserole by spread cabbage puree spread the warm layer mixture on top of the puree, top with a layer of shredded parmeshen cheese and sprinkle basil over it.
4. Place in oven and bake for 20 minutes at 375F and enjoy delicious taste with your friends or family.

Nutritional Information

- Preparation Time: 35 minutes
- Total servings: 6
- Calories: 330.5 (per serving)
- Fat: 29g
- Protein: 13.2g
- Carbs: 4.1g

RECIPE 9: MAPLE CHIA WAFFLES

Ingredients

Waffles:

- Chia flour ½ cup
- Chia seeds 1 ½ tbsp.
- Coconut milk ¼ cup
- Berry extract ½ tsp.
- Baking soda 1 tsp.
- Large eggs 2
- Ghee 2 tbsp.
- Stevia 10 drops

Filling:

- Maple syrup ¼ cup
- Lemon zest 2 tbsp.
- Ghee 2 tbsp.
- Swerve 1 tbsp.
- Cream ¼ cup

Topping: Pistachio flakes 2 tbsp.

Preparation Method

1. At first, mix all ingredients for the waffles in a container and mix until it looks smooth.
2. Add your batter to waffle maker or small pan and after cooking to allow them to cool. Lay cheese on top of your waffles while still warm.
3. In a pan, heat ghee and swerve on medium heat until it looks brown, now add your maple, orange zest.
4. Continue to stir the mixture until it bubbles and becomes like jam. On the other side, heat the waffle until brie start melting.
5. Now, add filling and cheese together and put on pan and grill for 1-2 per side and enjoy the taste with a little maple in the top.

Nutritional Information

- Preparation Time: 20 minutes
- Total servings: 12
- Calories: 511 (2 pieces per serving)
- Fat: 40.4g
- Protein: 20g
- Carbs: 7g

RECIPE 10: YUMMY CHIA PANCAKES

Ingredients

- Almond flour ½ cup
- Chia meal ½ cup
- Large eggs 4
- Maple syrup 2 tbsp.
- Avocado oil 4 tsp.
- Coconut milk ½ cup
- Erythritol 4 tsp.
- Ghee2 tbsp.
- Coconut flour 1 tsp.
- Baking powder1 tsp.
- Cinnamon ½ tsp.
- Salt to taste

Topping:

- Cherries 2 tbsp.
- Cashews 2 tbsp.

Preparation Method

1. At first, mix almond flour, chia seeds, Erythritol, salt and baking powder in bowl.
2. Mix all dry ingredients together well so everything is distributed evenly and add eggs to mixture and mix well.
3. Mix to a liquid consistency is achieved and add now avocado oil, maple syrup and milk together and mix until more liquid consistency.
4. Add coconut flour, spices to mixture and mix well. In a skillet, heat ghee and add ¼ cup of pancake mix at a time (try to cook 2 at a time).
5. Cook until brown color appears and remove from pan. Before serving, add little maple syrup and enjoy the taste.

Nutritional Information

- Preparation Time: 20 minutes
- Total servings: 8
- Calories: 241.5 (per serving)
- Fat: 25.5g
- Protein: 7.5g
- Carbs: 3.3g

KETOGENIC LUNCH RECIPES

RECIPE 11: SESAME LAYERED TURKEY CHICKEN

Ingredients

- Flax meal 1 ¼ cup
- Large eggs 2
- Turkey sausages 2
- Chicken sausages 2
- Vegetable oil 150ml (for frying)
- Heavy cream 1 oz.
- Allspice 1 tsp.
- Salt ½ tsp.
- Chili powder 1 tsp.
- BBQ sauce 2 tbsp.
- Toasted sesame seeds 2 tbsp.

Preparation Method

1. In a mixing bowl, add flax meal, allspice and mix all the dry ingredients well so they are completely distributed.
2. Add your eggs, baking soda and heavy cream to the batter and mix everything well until a nice thick batter is formed.
3. In a saucepan, heat vegetable oil to 400F. Cut each sausage into 2 pieces and mix half turkey and half chicken sausage into single sausage; dip mixed. Sausages in the batter before you fry them. Make sure they're fully coated
4. Drop your sausage into the oil 1 at a time. Let it cook for 5 minutes on one side, then flip it and cook for about 2 minutes on the other side.
5. Remove your sausages from the pan and let it dry on some paper towels. Sprinkle toasted sesame seeds over it the dish out with some hot sauces with hot BBQ sauce and enjoy the taste.

Nutritional Information

- Preparation Time: 10 minutes
- Serving per Recipe: 4
- Calories:382.3 (per serving)
- Fat: 36.7g
- Protein: 17g
- Carbs: 5.2g

RECIPE 12: ALMONDKIMCHI BOWL

Ingredients

- Halloumi cheese 2
- Kimchi 2 oz.
- Black sesame seeds 1 tsp.
- Almond flakes 3 tbsp.
- Chili flakes 1 tsp.
- Broccoli 2 tbsp.
- Mascarpone cheese 1 oz.

Sauce:

- Tahini 2 tbsp.
- Lemon juice 3 tbsp.
- Chili sauce 3 tbsp.
- Cayenne pepper 1 tsp.

Preparation Method

1. At first, combine sauce ingredients in a small bowl then stir until smooth and creamy (add more water to thin if desire).
2. Now, place the Halloumi cheese, mascarpone and kimchi in bowls then top with sauce, black sesame seeds, almond flakes and chili flakes.
3. Finally, enjoy the yummy bowl with delicious taste.

Nutritional Information

- Preparation Time: 15 minutes
- Total servings: 2
- Calories: 384 (per serving)
- Fat: 39.2g
- Protein: 16.7g
- Carbs: 5.2g

RECIPE 13: WINTER VEGETABLE STEW

Ingredients

- Winter vegetable mix 1 lb.
- Ghee 2 tbsp.
- Garlic powder 1 tsp.
- Ginger powder 1 tsp.
- Tomato puree1.5 oz.
- All spice 1 ½ tbsp.
- Paprika 1 ½ tsp.
- Salt to taste
- Diced tomatoes 7 oz.
- Coconut milk 1 cup
- Walnut paste 1 tbsp.
- Coriander1 ½ tbsp.

Topping:

- Grated mascarpone cheese

reparation Method

1. At first, mix chopped winter vegetables into bite sized pieces and season with salt, pepper and garlic, ginger and mix well.
2. Add canned diced tomatoes and tomato paste, mix well again then add coconut milk, walnut paste and mix well.
3. Cook for 35 minutes on medium heat. Before serving, add ghee, grated mascarpone and enjoy extra flavor taste.

Nutritional Information

- Preparation Time: 40 minutes
- Serving per Recipe: 5
- Calories: 566.8 (per serving)
- Fat: 46.6g
- Protein: 22.2g
- Carbs: 6.3g

RECIPE 14: GRILLED MASCARPONE SALMON

Ingredients

- Smoked salmon1 lb.
- Mascarpone cheese 2oz.
- Ghee 2 tbsp.
- Asparagus ½ stem
- Vinegar 2 tbsp.
- Thyme ½ tsp.
- Lavender ½ tsp.
- Basil ½ tsp.
- Thyme ½ tsp.
- Sea salt to taste

Preparation Method

1. At first, preheat your grill. Whisk ghee, vinegar, and herbs together.
2. Now, mix smoked salmon in herb mixture, it should cover both sides. Lay the smoked salmon on your preheated grill and cook for about 5 minutes on both sides.
3. Finally, add mascarpone cheese on top and grill for 1 minute or until cheese starts to melt then sprinkle sea salt and enjoy the taste.

Nutritional Information

- Preparation Time: 10 minutes
- Total servings: 4
- Calories: 171 (per serving)
- Fat: 13.2g
- Protein: 6.2g
- Carbs: 3.1g

RECIPE 15: RIND SQUASH ROLLS

Ingredients

Filling:

- Rind 4 oz.
- Celery 1 stalk
- Medium squash 1
- Ginger ½ tsp.
- Garlic ½ tsp.
- Maple syrup 1 tsp.
- Mascarpone cheese 2 oz.
- Stock powder 1 tsp.

Wrappers:

- Beaten egg 1
- Cornstarch 1 tsp.
- Spring roll wrappers 8
- Ghee 2 tsp.

Preparation Method

1. Filling: In a mixing bowl, add shredded rind, celery, squash, ginger, garlic, maple, stock powder, mascarpone and mix well until it mixes well.

2. On the other side, make a thick paste by mixing egg with the cornstarch and keep aside, then put some filling on each spring roll wrapper and slowly roll.

3. Roll it up with wet hands and seal the ends with the egg mixture.

4. Finally, preheat the oven to 390°F (198°C) and brush the spring rolls with little ghee and place on baking basket then cook for 10 minutes or until it turns to golden brown color.

5. If desired, serve with sweet chili sauce or Sriracha sauce to enjoy better taste.

Nutritional Information

- Preparation Time: 20 minutes
- Total servings: 4
- Calories: 377 (per serving)
- Fat: 24.7g
- Protein: 12.2g
- Carbs: 5g

RECIPE 16: BACON PEPPER OMELET

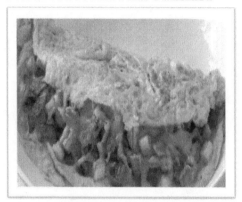

Ingredients

- Bacon 2 slices (cooked)
- Bacon fat 1 tbsp.
- Pepper 2 tbsp.
- Large eggs 2
- Ghee 1 tbsp
- Mascarpone cheese 2 tbsp.
- Parmesan cheese 1 tbsp.
- Thyme 2 stems
- Salt and pepper to taste

Preparation Method

1. Before heating pan, shred the cheese and cooked bacon and chop the thyme
2. Now heat the pan with bacon fat in medium low heat, add eggs, mint, salt and chopped pepper.
3. Once edges are starting to turn a light brown color, add bacon to the center of the pan and cook for 30 seconds by adding ghee on top.
4. Switch off pan and add cheese's on center and start folding from four sides of omelet slowly.
5. Now, turn the omelet and cook until it turns slightly golden color. Enjoy the delicious bacon omelet.

Nutritional Information

- Preparation Time: 15 minutes
- Total servings: 1
- Calories: 579 (per serving)
- Fat: 47.1g
- Protein: 22.9g
- Carbs: 5.3g

RECIPE 17: WILD BACON MUSHROOM

Ingredients

- Egg 1
- Bacon slices 2
- Wild mushrooms 1 oz.
- Sweet potato 2 oz.
- Yellow pepper 1 oz.
- Ghee 2 tbsp.
- Salt and pepper to taste
- Fresh thyme 1 tbsp.

Preparation Method

1. In a small pan, roast the wild mushrooms with ghee and season with salt, pepper. Keep aside.
2. Now, roast the bacon, sweet potato cubes, yellow pepper and keep aside. In the same pan, make an omelet with egg and garnish with freshly chopped thyme.
3. Finally, place all items on serving plate and enjoy the taste.

Nutritional Information

- Preparation Time: 15 minutes
- Total servings: 1
- Calories: 404 (per serving)
- Fat: 36g
- Protein: 15g
- Carbs: 6.1g

RECIPE 18: CHEESE CABBAGE SAUSAGE

Ingredients

- Sausage 1.5 oz.
- Cabbage 2 oz.
- Parmesan cheese 0.5 oz.
- Mascarpone cheese 1 oz.
- Mozzarella 0.5 oz.
- Oregano 1 tsp.
- Basil 1 tsp.
- Salt ½ tsp.
- Coriander paste 1 tsp.
- Red pepper ½ tsp.
- Ghee 2 tbsp.

Preparation Method

1. At first, preheat the oven to 350F. Place the skillet over medium heat and ghee.
2. When ghee is hot, add sausage, cook for 15 minutes and keep aside.
3. Meanwhile, slice cabbage and cook in skillet until it turns to golden brown color
4. Now, cut sausages into round slices and put back in skillet, add parmesan cheese, mascarpone cheese and stir once.
5. Your skillet into preheated oven for 15 minutes before you remove sprinkle grated mozzarella cheese and chopped herbs. Let it cool for 10 minutes and enjoy the taste.

Nutritional Information

- Preparation Time: 25 minutes
- Total servings: 1
- Calories: 599 (per serving)
- Fat: 47.7g
- Protein: 28.4g
- Carbs: 5.5g

KETOGENIC SALAD RECIPES

RECIPE 19: SWEET CHEESE DUCK SALAD

Ingredients

- Duck breasts 14 oz.
- Bacon slices 4 oz.
- Dates 2 (chopped)
- Romaine lettuce 1.76 lb.
- Salad Dressing 8 tbsp.
- Mascarpone cheese 4 oz.
- Salt and pepper to taste
- Anchovies 1 oz.

Preparation Method

1. At first, preheat your oven to 375F and bake bacons until it becomes crispy approximately 15 minutes and keep aside.
2. Now, make duck breast fry, by placing in oven to 430F, don't forget to season with salt and pepper. Cook for 15 minutes or until golden color and keep aside.
3. Meanwhile, prepare dressing and other ingredients. Use a peeler to make the mascarpone flakes, dates and place the lettuce in a serving bowl and toss with the dressing.
4. Now, slice the duck breasts into thin strips and place on top of the lettuce. Add the mascarpone flakes and crisped up and crumbled bacon, anchovies and enjoy the taste.

Nutritional Information

- Preparation Time: 45 minutes
- Total servings: 4
- Calories: 666 (per serving)
- Fat: 52.5g
- Protein: 28.6g
- Carbs: 7.1g

RECIPE 20: GREEN NUT SALAD

Ingredients

- Mixed greens 1 oz. (spinach, rapini, collards)
- Fresh herbs 1 oz. (Mint, Marjoram)
- Roasted pine nuts 1 oz.
- Pistachio 2 tbsp.
- Vinaigrette 1 ½ tbsp.
- Parmesan cheese 1 tbsp.
- Mascarpone cheese 1 tbsp.
- Bacon slices 2
- Ghee 1 tbsp.
- Salt and pepper to taste

Preparation Method

1. Cook bacon until crisp. Measure your greens, herbs and set in a container that can be shaken.
2. Crumble bacon, then add the rest of the ingredients to the greens and shake the container with a lid.
3. Add your seasonings and ghee for better taste and shake once again for proper dressing. Serve and enjoy the taste.

Nutritional Information

- Preparation Time: 10 minutes
- Total servings: 2
- Calories: 341 (per serving)
- Fat: 28.3g
- Protein: 11.2g
- Carbs: 5.2g

RECIPE 21: BOILED AVOCADO SALAD

Ingredients
- Large hard boiled eggs 4
- Avocado 150g
- Mayonnaise 1 tbsp.
- Fat yogurt 1 tbsp.
- Salt ½ tsp.
- Ghee 1 tbsp.
- Spring onions 1 tsp.
- Nuts 1 oz. (pistachio, brazil nuts)
- Mascarpone cheese 1 oz.
- Ground pepper to taste

Preparation Method
1. Combine avocado, mayonnaise, yogurt, salt and pepper. Combine with smashed egg and adjust salt and pepper as needed.
2. Sprinkle smashed nuts, spring onions, ghee, mascarpone cheese and enjoy the taste.

Nutritional Information
- Preparation Time: 10 minutes
- Total servings: 6
- Calories: 249.4 (per serving)
- Fat: 21.6g
- Protein: 9.3g
- Carbs: 4.1g

RECIPE 22: CHEESY ASPARAGUS SALAD

Ingredients

- Asparagus 2 oz. (cooked)
- Pine nuts 1 oz. (roasted)
- Vinaigrette 4 tsp.
- Parmesan cheese 1 tbsp.
- Mascarpone cheese 1 oz.
- Bacon 2 slices
- Salt and pepper to taste

Preparation Method

1. Cook bacon until crisp. Measure your asparagus and set in a container that can be shaken.
2. Crumble bacon, then add the rest of the ingredients to the beans and shake the container with a lid.
3. Add your seasonings for better taste and shake once again for proper dressing.
4. Before serving, add mozzarella balls and enjoy the taste.

Nutritional Information

- Preparation Time: 10 minutes
- Serving per Recipe: 1
- Calories: 534 (per serving)
- Fat: 40.7g
- Protein: 18.1g
- Carbs:6.2g

RECIPE 23: CRAB CARROT SALAD

Ingredients

- Carrot1 cup
- Crab meat 4 oz.
- Lemon juice 1 tbsp.
- Grape tomatoes 4
- Mascarpone 1 oz.
- Ghee 1 oz.
- Salt and pepper to taste
- Butter salad leaves 2
- Macadamia nuts 1 oz.

Preparation Method

1. In a medium bowl, add lemon juice, tomato, ghee, salt and fresh pepper. Add crab meat and sway lightly.
2. Cut the carrot and season with the remaining ingredients, mix carrot, crab and sprinkle smashed macadamia nuts. Serve immediately with butter leaves to enjoy the taste.

Nutritional Information

- Preparation Time: 15 minutes
- Total servings: 2
- Calories: 206 (per serving)
- Fat: 27g
- Protein: 13.2g
- Carbs:6.6g

RECIPE 24: TURKEY SALAD

Ingredients

- Spinach 2 oz.
- Dandelion greens ½ oz.
- Roasted Brazil nuts 1 oz.
- Vinaigrette 4 tsp.
- Grated cheese 1 tbsp.
- Mozzarella cheese 1 oz.
- Turkey slices 2 (each 1 oz.)
- Salt and pepper to taste

Preparation Method

1. Cook turkey until crisp. Measure your greens and set in a container that can be shaken.
2. Crumble bacon, then add the rest of the ingredients to the greens and shake the container with a lid.
3. Add your seasonings for better taste and shake once again for proper dressing.
4. Before serving, add mozzarella balls and enjoy the taste.

Nutritional Information

- Preparation Time: 10 minutes
- Serving per Recipe: 1
- Calories: 553 (per serving)
- Fat: 36.4g
- Protein: 16.6g
- Carbs: 7g

RECIPE 25: CHICKENDILL SALAD

Ingredients

- Mixed green 2 oz.
- Roasted macadamia nuts 1 oz.
- Vinaigrette 4 tsp.
- Parmesan cheese 1 tbsp.
- Chicken breast 2 slices
- Dill 1 tbsp.
- Salt and pepper (as required)

Preparation Method

1. Cook chicken until crispy. Measure your greens and put in a container that can be shaken.
2. Crumble chicken, then add the rest of the ingredients to the greens and shake the container with a lid.
3. Add your spices for better taste, chopped dill and slate once again for proper dressing. Serve and enjoy the taste.

Nutritional Information

- Preparation Time: 10 minutes
- Total servings: 1
- Calories: 344 (per serving)
- Fat: 30.5g
- Protein: 14.3g
- Carbs: 4.5g

RECIPE 26: GOJI SALAD

Ingredients

- Goji berries 5 oz.
- Goat cheese 5 oz.
- Rinds 1 oz.
- Pecans 2 oz.
- Fresh red lettuce 4 oz.
- Ghee 2 tbsp.
- Balsamic vinegar 1 tbsp.

Preparation Method
1. At first, powder the rinds using a blender and keep aside.
2. Now, cut each goat cheese in circular shape. Apply ghee and cover in powdered pork rinds. Place in freezer for 60 minutes to prevent the cheese from melting when grilled.
3. Meanwhile, preheated your grill to 450F and cook cheese for just about 5 minutes.
4. On other hand, wash Goji berries, spray vinegar and place in oven at 450F for 10 minutes.
5. Place washed lettuce in a serving bowl and add roasted pecans, drizzle the salad with ghee.
6. Add the Goji berries, grilled cheese to salad and enjoy your meal.

Nutritional Information
- Preparation Time: 75 minutes
- Total servings: 2
- Calories: 599 (per serving)
- Fat: 44.5g
- Protein: 21.8g
- Carbs: 6.3g

RECIPE 27: MIXED SQUASH SALAD

Ingredients

- Fresh tomato 1
- Mixed squash 3 oz. (Butter squash, Acorn, Yellow squash)
- Fresh mozzarella cheese 6 oz.
- Turnip greens 1 tbsp.
- Fresh thyme 1 ½ tbsp.
- Ghee 3 tbsp.
- Mascarpone cheese 2 tbsp.
- Vinegar 1 tbsp.
- Fresh black pepper to taste
- Himalaya salt to taste

Preparation Method
1. In a food processor, put chopped fresh basil, turnip leaves with ghee to make the paste.
2. Slice tomato into 1/4" slices. You should be able to get at least 6 slices from the tomato and mixed squash.
3. Cut mozzarella, mascarpone into slices. Assemble salad by layering tomato, mozzarella, and paste.
4. Season with salt, pepper, and remaining ghee and enjoy the taste.

Nutritional Information
- Preparation Time: 12 minutes
- Serving per Recipe: 2
- Calories:339 (per serving)
- Fat: 40.1g
- Protein: 15.9g
- Carbs: 6.6g

KETOGENIC SOUP RECIPES

RECIPE 28: BACON BROCCOLI SOUP

Ingredients
- Vegetable broth 1 ½ cups
- Bacon4 slices
- Broccoli puree 1 cup
- Ghee1 oz.
- Butter 1 oz.
- Garlic 1 tsp.
- Ginger 1 tsp.
- Salt ½ tsp.
- Pepper ½ tsp.
- Red chili flakes 2
- Fresh ginger ½ tsp.
- Mint ¼ tsp.
- Bay leaf 1
- Mascarpone cheese 1 oz.

Preparation Method
1. Keep saucepan over medium heat, add ghee. When ghee is hot, add garlic and fresh ginger.
2. Let this sauté for about 3 minutes or until onions start to go translucent then add spices (salt, pepper, coriander, bay leaf, red chili flakes) to the pan and let cook for 2 minutes. Add broccoli puree to pan and stir into the onions and spices well
3. Once the broccoli is mixed well, add vegetable broth to the pan. Stir until everything is combined.
4. Bring to a boil to simmer for 20 minutes. Once simmered, use an immersion blender to blend together all of the ingredients. You want a smooth puree here so make sure you take your time. Cook for an additional 20 minutes.
5. In the meantime, cook 4 slices of bacon over medium heat. Once the soup is ready, pour mascarpone cheese and the grease from the cooked bacon and mix well.
6. Crumble the bacon over the top of the soup and enjoy the taste of the soup.

Nutritional Information
- Preparation Time: 45 minutes
- Serving per Recipe: 3
- Calories:491 (per serving)
- Fat: 45.1g
- Protein: 10.8g
- Carbs: 5.7g

RECIPE 29: SOY LAMB SOUP

Ingredients

- Lamb bone1 lb.
- Onion Powder 1 tsp.
- Garlic Powder 1 tsp.
- Ginger powder 1 tsp.
- Chili powder ½ tsp.
- Ghee 2 oz.
- Soy sauce 2 oz.
- Broth 3 cups
- Cream cheese 2 oz.
- Cumin powder 1 tsp.
- Salt and Pepper to taste

Preparation Method

1. Cut or slice the lamb bones into chunks and drop them in the pot and add all the rest of the ingredients to the cooking pot except cream, cheese.
2. Set cooking pot on heat for 60 minutes and cooks completely. Once everything is cooked, remove the lamb from the cooking pot and shred using a fork.
3. Add cream and cheese to the cooking pot. Using an immersion blender, emulsify all of the liquids together. This will help the soup from separating while you are eating.
4. Place the lamb back into the cooking pot, stir together. Taste and season with extra salt, pepper, cumin and soy sauce. Serve and enjoy the taste.

Nutritional Information

- Preparation Time: 190 minutes
- Serving per Recipe: 5
- Calories:531.2 (per serving)
- Fat: 46.3g
- Protein: 22.1g
- Carbs: 5.4g

RECIPE 30: LAMB SAUSAGE SOUP

Ingredients

- Ground lamb 1 lb.
- Sausage 7 oz.
- Fresh tomatoes 7 oz.
- Tomato Puree 2 oz.
- Onions 2 oz.
- Garlic 3 cloves
- Ginger powder ½ tsp.
- Ghee 4 tbsp.
- Salt and pepper to taste
- Broth 1 liter
- Garnish with sweet marjoram

Preparation Method

1. At first, dice the onion, sausage, tomatoes and keep aside.
2. Place large Dutch pan over medium heat with ghee. Once ghee hot, add the diced onion, garlic, ginger and cook 2 minutes or until lightly browned, cook for 5 minutes, don't forget to stir to prevent burning.
3. Add the sausage, ground lamb into the pot and cook until it turns to brown color. Add the chopped tomatoes, tomato puree.
4. Now, add broth (your choice) and season with salt and pepper. Cook the soup until bubbles appears and before serving, add chopped sweet marjoram for extra flavor.

Nutritional Information

- Preparation Time: 30 minutes
- Total servings: 5
- Calories: 371 (per serving)
- Fat: 32g
- Protein: 15.3g
- Carbs: 6.1g

RECIPE 31: RED CHARDCHEESE SOUP

Ingredients

- Ghee 1 tbsp.
- Onion 1 oz.
- Red chard10 oz.
- Large eggs 8
- Goat cheese 8 oz.
- Mascarpone cheese 2 oz.
- Sea salt 1 tsp.
- Black pepper ½ tsp.

Preparation Method
1. At first, preheat your oven to 350F and place your pan over medium heat. When ghee is hot, add onions and cook until it becomes soft.
2. Add chopped chard and cook for 2 minutes and keep aside. In a bowl, mix egg, goat cheese, mascarpone, salt, pepper and add to mixture.
3. Using blender, blend the mixture and pour into pan, place in preheated oven for 30 minutes and enjoy the taste.

Nutritional Information
- Preparation Time: 40 minutes
- Total servings: 4
- Calories: 580 (per serving)
- Fat: 48g
- Protein: 27.1g
- Carbs: 6.9g

RECIPE 32: TURKEY GHEE SOUP

Ingredients
- Turkey leg 2 lb.
- Broth 240 ml
- Tomatoes 1 oz.
- Cream 1 oz.
- Ghee 1 oz.
- Garlic paste 1 tsp.
- Ginger paste 1 tsp.
- Chili powder 1 tsp.
- Mascarpone 1 oz.
- Sesame seeds 1 tsp. (toasted)
- Salt and pepper to taste
- Thyme 1 tsp.

Preparation Method

1. At first, preheat the oven to 375F, add ghee to the turkey, salt, pepper and place the marinated turkey in the oven for 25 minutes.

2. Cut mascarpone into small cubes pieces and set aside and heat the pan over medium heat and add ghee. When the ghee starts to brown, add ginger, garlic and mix for 2 minutes.

3. Add tomato, sesame seeds, chili powder and salt. Mix well all together. Add broth and let it simmer for 10 minutes and add cream, slowly stir in the medium heat.

4. Add turkey legs pieces gently into the sauce and let it boil for 5 minutes. Garnish with dill and enjoy the taste.

Nutritional Information

- Preparation Time: 35 minutes
- Total servings: 4
- Calories: 482 (per serving)
- Fat: 43g
- Protein: 16.1g
- Carbs: 4.4g

KETOGENIC DINNER RECIPES

RECIPE 33: COCONUT PORK STEW

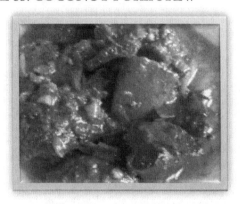

Ingredients

- Pork 1 lb.
- Ghee 1 oz.
- Onion powder 1 tbsp.
- Garlic powder 2 tsp.
- Ginger powder 1 tsp.
- All spice 1 tsp.
- Salt to taste
- Diced tomatoes 2 oz.
- Coconut milk4 oz.
- Parsley 1 tbsp.

Preparation Method

1. Cut the pork into small cube size pieces and season with salt, pepper and ground pepper, ginger, garlic and mix well.
2. Add tomatoes and mix well. Finally, add coconut milk and mix.
3. Cook for 40 minutes on medium heat and mix thoroughly then sprinkle chopped parsley. Serve over cauliflower rice or normal rice for nice taste.

Nutritional Information

- Preparation Time: 45 minutes
- Total servings: 5
- Calories: 501 (per serving)
- Fat: 40.8g
- Protein: 25.5g
- Carbs:5g

RECIPE 34: CHEESY KUMATOSANDWICH

Ingredients

- Kumato2 lb.
- Onions slices 1 oz.
- Ghee 2 tbsp.
- Ginger garlic paste 1 tbsp.
- Salt and black pepper to taste
- Mozzarella 7 oz.
- Mascarpone cheese 3 oz.
- Prawns1 oz. (cooked)
- Peanut butter 1 tbsp.
- Fresh rosemary 2 branches

Preparation Method

1. At first, preheat your oven at 450F. Slice the bottom of each kumato so that the kumato sit upright. Halve in each case.
2. Cut the kumatoshalves, cut on a foil-filled, flat frying pan or a baked sheet. Apply ghee to kumatos. Season with salt, pepper and sprinkle chopped garlic ginger paste over the tomatoes then fill onions in it.
3. Fry until softened and heated by, about 15 minutes. Meanwhile, cut the mozzarella, mascarpone, and prawns into slices. Using a spatula, sandwich each slice between 2 hot tomato halves and apply peanut butter (heat melts the cheese slightly).
4. Nourish the kumatos with juices collected in the frying pan and served with the fresh rosemary.

Nutritional Information

- Preparation Time: 20 minutes
- Total servings: 6 pieces
- Calories: 255.8(per serving)
- Fat: 20.5g
- Protein: 10g
- Carbs: 5g

RECIPE 35: FOREST MUSHROOM BROCCOLI BOWL

Ingredients

- Macadamia nuts ½ cup
- Coriander 2 cups
- Ginger paste 2 tsp.
- Lemon juice 2 tbsp.
- Salt and pepper to taste
- Mascarpone cheese 3 oz.
- Forest mushrooms 1 lb.
- Broccoli 2 oz.
- Ghee 1 tbsp.

Preparation Method

1. At first, soak macadamia nuts overnight in water then drain water and add macadamia nuts,

coriander, ginger, lemon juice, salt, and pepper to food processor then process until smooth.

2. Now, cook broccoli in small pan over medium heat for 10 minutes and keep aside then place large skillet over medium heat with ghee and add forest mushrooms, season with salt and pepper then cook for 10 minutes, don't forget to stir occasionally until all the water has evaporated and they begin to brown and keep aside.

3. Finally, add broccoli, a quarter of the forest mushrooms, mascarpone and top with a tablespoon of the pesto in bowl and enjoy the delicious taste.

Nutritional Information

- Preparation Time: 35 minutes
- Total servings: 4
- Calories: 381 (per serving)
- Fat: 34.4g
- Protein: 15.3g
- Carbs:7g

RECIPE 36: WINTER CHEESE SANDWICH

Ingredients

- Winter squash35 oz.
- Mozzarella 8 oz.
- Mascarpone cheese 2 oz.
- Ghee2 tbsp.
- Mint paste 2 tbsp.
- Chili powder 1 tbsp.
- Salt and black pepper to taste
- Prawns2 oz. (cooked)
- Fennel powder 1 tbsp.
- Cream ½ cup

Preparation Method
1. At first, preheat oven at 450F. Slice a thin slice each winter squash into 3 pieces and place in a flat frying pan or a baked sheet.
2. Apply ghee to summer squash. Season with salt, pepper and sprinkle chili powder over the sliced squash. Fry until softened and heated by, about 15 minutes.
3. Meanwhile, cut the mozzarella, mascarpone, prawns into six ½-inch thick slices. Using a spatula, sandwich each slice between 2 hot squash halves and apply mint, cream. Before serving, garnish with fennel powder and enjoy the taste.

Nutritional Information
- Preparation Time: 20 minutes
- Total servings: 3 pieces
- Calories: 254 (per serving)
- Fat: 23.7g
- Protein: 10.6g
- Carbs: 5.1g

RECIPE 37: ROASTED WALNUT TUNA FILET

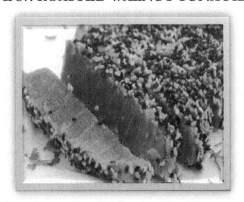

Ingredients

- Walnut 1 oz.
- Tuna fillet 1 lb.
- Halloumi cheese 2 oz. (grilled)
- Maple syrup 2 tbsp.
- Roasted mustard seeds ½ tsp.
- Thyme 1 tsp.
- Ghee 2 tbsp.
- Baby spinach 1 cup (steamed)
- Salt and pepper to taste

Preparation Method

1. At first, preheat your oven to 350F. Add walnuts, maple syrup, your spices and mustard in the mixer and make a paste.
2. Rub tuna with ghee and add the walnut paste to the top of the tuna fillets.
3. Transfer them to an oven cooking basket and bake for about 15 minutes. Serve with a little fresh baby spinach, halloumi cheese and a little smoked paprika. Enjoy the delicious taste.

Nutritional Information

- Preparation Time: 25 minutes
- Total servings: 2
- Calories: 364 (per serving)
- Fat: 22.4g
- Protein: 12g
- Carbs: 4.9g

RECIPE 38: MASCARPONE SALMON WRAPS

Ingredients

- Large eggs 3
- Avocado 3.5 oz.
- Smoked salmon 2 oz.
- Mascarpone cheese 2 tbsp.
- Fresh dill 2 tbsp.
- Cabbage 4 tbsp.
- Ghee 1 tbsp.
- Salt and pepper to taste

Preparation Method

1. At first, whisk egg, salt and pepper in a small bowl, add mascarpone cheese with chopped dill and keep aside.
2. Place pan over medium heat and add ghee, cabbage. When ghee is hot, add egg mixture into pan and cook for 1 minute each side.
3. Meanwhile, slice the smoked salmon, avocado and keep aside. Now, place the omelet on a plate and add sliced salmon, avocado and fold into a wrap.

Nutritional Information

- Preparation Time: 15 minutes
- Total servings: 2
- Calories: 388.7 (per serving)
- Fat: 34.6g
- Protein: 16.6g
- Carbs: 4.2g

RECIPE 39: TUNA OMELET

Ingredients

- Eggs 12
- Ghee 2 oz.
- Tuna 4 oz.
- Kale 2 oz.
- Mascarpone cheese 2 oz.
- Mozzarella cheese 2 oz.
- Garlic 2 tsp.
- Parmesan cheese 2 oz.
- All spice 1 tsp.
- Salt and pepper to taste

Preparation Method

1. Frozen kale in the microwave oven for 3 minutes and drain the water and set aside.
2. Preheat oven to 375F. In a large bowl, add eggs, ghee, spices and beat well until everything is well combined.
3. Add parmesan, mascarpone, kale and mix well by adding little water, then sprinkle mozzarella cheese over the top and add tuna over it.
4. Bake for 30 minutes or until completely cooked properly. Slice and enjoy the taste.

Nutritional Information

- Preparation Time: 60 minutes
- Total servings: 8
- Calories: 343.1 (per serving)
- Fat: 27g
- Protein: 15.5g
- Carbs: 4.1g

RECIPE 40: COCONUT TURKEYSTEW

Ingredients

- Onions 2 oz.
- Garlic powder 1 tsp.
- Ginger powder 1 tsp.
- Ghee 2 tsp.
- Turkey1 lb.
- Coconut milk 1 cup
- Parsley1 tbsp.
- Cumin powder 1 tsp.
- Green chili 1 tsp.
- Turmeric 1 tsp.
- Frozen black beans2 oz.
- Brazil nuts 2 oz.
- Tomato sauce 1 oz.
- Salt and fresh pepper to taste

Preparation Method
1. Heat in a large skillet pan; add ghee and onions on medium heat. Cook about 10 minutes. Add garlic and ginger, cook for another 2 minutes.
2. Add lamb to the pan and brown. Season with salt, pepper, cumin, coriander, green chili, turmeric and mix well.
3. Add coconut milk, brazil nuts, tomato sauce and water. Reduce heat to simmer about 20 minutes. Add frozen peas and simmer for an additional 15 minutes or until desired taste comes.

Nutritional Information
- Preparation Time: 35 minutes
- Total servings: 4
- Calories: 380.3 (per serving)
- Fat: 32.6g
- Protein: 17.2g
- Carbs: 8g

RECIPE 41: VINAIGRETTE LAMB FRY

Ingredients

Lamb Chops

- Lamb chops 4
- Ghee 1 oz.
- Salt and pepper to taste
- Paprika 1 tsp.
- Small better melon 1
- Catnip 1 tsp.

Vinaigrette

- Vinegar 2 tbsp.
- Lemon juice 1 tbsp.
- Maple syrup 1 tbsp.
- Salt and pepper to taste

Topping

- Parsley 1 tbsp.

Preparation Method
1. At first, season lamb chops with salt, pepper, ghee and keep aside.
2. Place large iron skillet over high heat and add seasoned lamb chops and cook 10 minutes both side.
3. Decrease the heat to medium and add better melon slices, catnip over the lamb chops and place in the oven for about 10 minutes at 350F.
4. Meanwhile, prepare vinaigrette by mixing all the ingredients together. When lamb chops are ready, pour vinaigrette over top then sprinkle parsley and serve hot.

Nutritional Information
- Preparation Time: 25 minutes
- Total servings: 2
- Calories: 488 (per serving)
- Fat: 40.7g
- Protein: 21.3g
- Carbs: 5.3g

RECIPE 42: BACON CHEESE LAYER

Ingredients

- Bacon 4 oz.
- Mozzarella cheese 5 oz.
- Cheddar cheese 3.5 oz.
- Mascarpone cheese 3 oz.
- Coconut flour 4 tbsp.
- Chia meal 3 tbsp.
- Egg yolk 1
- Herb seasoning 1 tsp.
- Salt and pepper to taste

Preparation Method

1. At first, preheat the oven to 400F and in a microwave or toaster oven, melt your mozzarella cheese. About 1 minute in the microwave, and 10second intervals afterward, or about 10 minutes in an oven, stirring occasionally.
2. In a mixing bowl, mix chia meal, herb seasonings, salt, pepper, mozzarella (melted), mascarpone, egg yolk and make moist dough, transfer it to a flat surface with some parchment paper.
3. Using rolling pin flatten dough and using knife cut diagonal lines beginning from the edges of the dough to the center, leave a row of dough untouched about 4 inches wide.
4. Alternate lay bacon slices and cheddar on that uncut stretch of dough then cover your filling by lift one section of dough at a time and lay it over the top.
5. Finally, bake in preheated oven for 20 minutes until you see it has turned a golden brown color and enjoy the taste.

Nutritional Information

*   Preparation Time: 40 minutes
*   Total servings: 4
*   Calories: 343 (per serving)
*   Fat: 37.4g
*   Protein: 24.2g
*   Carbs: 5.4g

RECIPE 43: SUMMER BACON FRY

Ingredients

- Summer squash 7 oz.
- Bacon 2 oz.
- Onions 1 oz.
- Garlic clove 2
- Ghee 1 tbsp.
- Fresh parsley 1 tbsp.
- Salt ¼ tsp.

Preparation Method

1. At first, chop onions, garlic, and bacon and add it to large skillet over a medium heat and cook until it turns light brown color.
2. On the other hand, dice the summer squash into medium cube size pieces and add to skillet, cook for 15 minutes. Don't forget to stir frequently and finally add chopped parsley.

Nutritional Information

- Preparation Time: 25 minutes
- Total servings: 1
- Calories: 411 (per serving)
- Fat: 34.1g
- Protein: 17g
- Carbs: 6.2g

KETOGENIC SNACK RECIPES

RECIPE 44: CABBAGE BISCUITS

Ingredients
- Almond flour 1 ½ cup
- Cabbage1.5 lb.
- Cheddar cheese 5 oz.
- Mascarpone cheese 4 oz.
- Ghee 2 oz.
- Large eggs 2
- Salt to taste
- Ginger powder 1 tsp.
- Baking soda ½ tsp.
- Chopped walnuts 2 tbsp.

Preparation Method

1. At first, preheat your oven to 375F, blend cabbage until it is finely chopped.
2. In a large bowl, mix almond flour, salt, peppers, ginger powder, baking soda. Mix it well, add eggs and ghee. Mix until a dough forms.
3. Add your cabbage to the mixture. Combine everything with your hands. Grate cheddar and mascarpone to the dough. Mix everything with the hands until the cheese is evenly distributed.
4. Place your non-stick slat on a cookie sheet, so that they do not stick as they boil. Form pies from the dough and sprinkle chopped walnuts. Bake like biscuits for 15 minutes or until they begin to flatten.
5. Turn it and continue baking for about 5 minutes then, turn your oven to roast and brew the biscuits for 3 minutes. Let it cool for 2 minutes before you enjoy the taste.

Nutritional Information

- Preparation Time: 30 minutes
- Total servings: 12
- Calories: 189 (per serving)
- Fat: 17.8g
- Protein: 7g
- Carbs: 3.1g

RECIPE 45: BANANA BOMBS

Ingredients

- Ghee 4 oz.
- Heavy whipped cream 4 oz.
- Fresh cheese 4 oz.
- Vanillas extract1 tsp.
- Stevia 10 drops
- Banana protein powder 1 oz.

Preparation Method
1. At first, mix ghee, heavy cream and fresh cheese. Using a mixer, mix all the ingredients together or place in microwave oven for 30 seconds to 1 minute to soften them.
2. Add berry extract and liquid stevia to the mixture and mix with a spoon.
3. Distribute the mixture into a silicone tray and freeze for 3 hours.

Nutritional Information
- Preparation Time: 182 minutes
- Total servings: 10
- Calories: 186 (per serving)
- Fat: 18g
- Protein: 7.9g
- Carbs: 1g

RECIPE 46: CHIA CHEESECAKE

Ingredients

Brownie Bottom:

- Ghee4 oz.
- Chocolate 2 oz.
- Chia flour ½ cup
- Cocoa powder 2 oz.
- Pinch of salt
- Large eggs 2
- Sweetener 2 oz.
- Pistachios1 oz.

Cheesecake filling:

- Fresh cheese 1 lb.
- Large eggs 2
- Swerve sweetener 3 oz.
- Heavy cream 2 oz.
- Pineapple extracts ½ tsp.

Preparation Method

1. For the brownie base, preheat the oven to 325F and butter a 9 inch pan form pan. Wrap bottom of the pan with foil.

2. In a microwaveable bowl or glass measuring cup, melt ghee and chocolate together in the microwave in 30 seconds steps. Snow bees to smooth. Alternatively, you can melt them together at low heat in a small pot.

3. In a small bowl, beat chia flour, cocoa powder and salt. In a large bowl, beat eggs, sweetener and vanilla until smooth. Beat in chia flour mixture and then ghee chocolate mixture until smooth. Stir in nuts.

4. Spread evenly over the bottom of the prepared pan. Bake 20 minutes, until around the edges, but still soft in the middle. Leave to cool for 15 minutes.

5. For the filling, reduce the oven temperature to 300F. In a large bowl, beat fresh cheese until smooth. Beat in eggs, sweetener, and cream until well combined.

6. Pour filling over crust and square cheesecake on a large biscuit sheet. Bake until the edges are set and the center wiggles only slightly, 45 minutes. Remove from oven and allow cooling.

7. Run a knife to release the edges and then remove the sides of the pan. Cover with plastic film and store in refrigerator for at least 3 hours. Serve with sugar-free chocolate sauce.

Nutritional Information

- Preparation Time: 80 minutes
- Total servings: 10
- Calories: 393 (per serving)
- Fat: 34.8g
- Protein: 8.9g
- Carbs: 4.4g

RECIPE 47: CRUNCHY CHIA BISCUITS

Ingredients

- Chia flour 1 ½ cup
- Ghee 2 oz.
- Salt to taste
- Baking soda ½ tsp.
- Cayenne pepper ¼ tsp.
- Garlic powder 1 tsp.
- Ginger powder 1 tsp.
- Thyme2 tbsp.

Preparation Method

1. At first, preheat oven to 325F. Place a cookie sheet with parchment paper.
2. In a medium bowl, mix chia flour, pepper, salt and baking powder.
3. Add thyme, cayenne and garlic, ginger and stir until uniformly combined. Next, add to the pesto and snow bake until the dough forms into coarse crumbs.
4. Put the ghee into the cracker mixture with a fork until the dough forms a ball.
5. Transfer the dough to the prepared cookie sheet and spread the dough thinly until it is about 1 mm thick. Make sure the thickness is the same, so that the biscuits evenly bake.
6. Place the pan in the pre-heated oven then sprinkle thyme over it and bake for 15 minutes to light golden brown color. After baking, remove from the oven and cut into biscuits of the desired size.

Nutritional Information

- Preparation Time: 25 minutes
- Total servings: 6
- Calories:226 (per serving)
- Fat: 21g
- Protein: 5.3g
- Carbs: 2.5g

RECIPE 48: ENERGY PEANUT BARS

Ingredients
- Coconut butter 1 cup
- Pumpkin purees 1 cup
- Ground cinnamon 1 tbsp.
- Peanuts 1 oz.
- Peanut butter 3 oz..
- Protein powder 2 oz.
- Ghee2 tbsp.

Preparation Method

1. Hold aside 8x8 inch square baking tray with aluminum foil. In the large bowl, add melted coconut butter, peanut butter, pumpkin puree, spices, protein powder and mix well.
2. Add ghee and combine well without lumps. Pour the mixture into the already prepared pan and spread evenly then sprinkle chopped peanuts.
3. Cover with wax paper and evenly put into the pan. Remove wax paper and place the mixture in the refrigerator for 3 hours.
4. Use a sharp knife to cut into 25 equal squares and enjoy the delicious taste.

Nutritional Information

- Preparation Time: 15 minutes
- Total servings: 25
- Calories: 177 (per serving)
- Fat: 15.9g
- Protein: 7.7g
- Carbs: 2.6g

RECIPE 49: DURIAN MUG CAKE

Ingredients

- Durian 0.7 oz.
- Almond flour 2 tbsp.
- Chia flour 1 tbsp.
- Baking soda ⅛ tsp.
- Swerve 1 tbsp.
- Large egg 1
- Berry extracts ½ tsp.
- Ghee 1 tbsp.
- Whipped cream 2 tbsp.

Preparation Method

1. At first, place all the dry ingredients in a mug and combine well. Top with chopped durian.
2. Place mug in microwave on high for 90 seconds. Before serving add whipping cream and enjoy the taste.

Nutritional Information

- Preparation Time: 3 minutes
- Total servings: 1
- Calories: 349 (per serving)
- Fat: 24.9g
- Protein: 11.8g
- Carbs: 4.7g

RECIPE 50: PROTEIN FLAX BARS

Ingredients

- Flax ½ cup
- Ghee 2 oz.
- Maple syrup 1 oz.
- Cinnamon powder 1 tsp.
- Pinch of salt
- Cashew nuts 2 oz.
- Cashew butter 1 oz.
- Protein powder 2 oz.
- Shredded coconut 1 tbsp.

Preparation Method
1. At first, combine flax and melted ghee in a large bowl. Add cinnamon, salt and maple syrup, cashew butter, protein powder and mix well.
2. Add chopped cashews and mix everything evenly. Pour parchment paper into a casserole dish and spread the dough in a flat layer. Sprinkle crushed coconut and cinnamon up for beautiful crispy flavor.
3. Place them in a refrigerator and cool for 3 hours (night will give the best result). Cut into bars and enjoy the taste.

Nutritional Information
- Preparation Time:15 minutes
- Total servings: 8
- Calories: 199.5 (per serving)
- Fat: 21.7g
- Protein: 9.3g
- Carbs: 4.6g

KETOGENIC SMOOTHIE RECIPES

RECIPE 51: COCO-CREAM SMOOTHIE

Ingredients
- Coconut butter 2 tablespoons
- Coconut Milk 60ml
- Heavy whipping cream 60g
- Egg white protein powder 24g
- Extra virgin coconut oil 1 tablespoon
- Cacao powder 1 tablespoon
- Stevia extract 5 drops
- Water 60ml
- Ice 100ml
- Cinnamon 2g
- Vanilla extract 5 drops

Preparation Method

1. Add all ingredients into the blender and blend until smooth
2. Pour into glass and enjoy the taste with straw

Nutritional Info

- Preparation Time: 05 minutes
- Serving per Recipe: 1
- Calories: 570
- Protein: 34.5g
- Fat: 46g
- Carbohydrates: 6.2g

RECIPE 52: RASPBERRY CHEESE SMOOTHIE

Ingredients
- Cream cheese 60g
- Coconut milk 60ml
- Raspberries 40g
- Cocoa powder 5g
- Water 120ml
- Extra virgin coconut oil 14g

Preparation Method
1. Add all ingredients into the blender and blend until smooth
2. Pour into glass and enjoy the taste with straw

Nutritional Info
- Preparation Time: 5 minutes
- Serving per Recipe: 1
- Calories: 512 (per serving)
- Protein:6.9 g
- Fat: 53.6g
- Carbohydrates: 7g

RECIPE 53: ALMOND HORCHATA SMOOTHIE

Ingredients

- Almonds blanched 60g
- Almond milk 240ml
- Egg 1
- Ground chia seeds 16g
- Lime zest 10g
- Cinnamon 4g
- Erythritol 30g
- Stevia 20 drops
- Warm water 480ml

Preparation Method

1. In blender, place all ingredients and blend on medium speed or until smooth
2. Pour into serving glass and enjoy the taste

Nutritional Info

- Preparation Time: 5 minutes
- Serving per Recipe: 2
- Calories: 282 (per serving)
- Protein: 11.9g
- Fat: 22.2g
- Carbohydrates: 5g

RECIPE 54: PUMPKIN SMOOTHIE

Ingredients
- Pumpkin puree 50g
- Almond milk 60ml
- Egg white protein powder 25g
- Coconut milk 60g
- Pumpkin pie spice mix 2g
- Stevia 3 drops
- Extra virgin coconut oil 14g
- Topping: coconut cream 15g

Preparation Method
1. In blender, place all ingredients and blend on medium speed or until smooth
2. Pour into serving glass and top with coconut cream

Nutritional Info

- Preparation Time: 5 minutes
- Serving per Recipe: 1
- Calories: 399 (per serving)
- Protein: 21.8g
- Fat: 32.6g
- Carbohydrates: 6.7g

RECIPE 55: VANILLA CREAM SMOOTHIE

Ingredients
- Almond butter 30g
- Soured cream 115g
- Plain whey protein 25g
- Extra virgin coconut oil 14g
- Vanilla extract 5g
- Stevia 5 drops
- Water 60ml
- Ice cube 50ml

Preparation Method

1. In blender, place all ingredients and blend on medium speed or until smooth
2. Pour into serving glass and enjoy the taste

Nutritional Info

- Preparation Time:5 minutes
- Serving per Recipe: 1
- Calories: 566 (per serving)
- Protein: 34.6g
- Fat: 45.2g
- Carbohydrates: 5.1g

CONCLUSION: MY EXPERIENCE AND WHAT YOU WANT TO KNOW

Turning your body right into a fat-burning system has obvious blessings for weight reduction. Fat burning is vastly elevated even as insulin, this creates best situations in which fat loss can arise, without starvation. Overall benefits that you are going to get are:

- Rapid weight loss
- Type 2 diabetes reversed
- Increased mental focus
- Improved physical endurance
- Metabolic syndrome
- Epilepsy controlling
- Decreasing cancers
- Controlled blood pressure
- Less stomach problems
- Acne control
- Decreasing heartburn
- Decreasing migraine attacks
- Decreasing sugar cravings
- Reverse PCOS

How can the reader apply what the learned right away?

For a few humans, it's far very smooth to drop a sizable amount of weight on keto diet in less time. Normally a weight reduction stabilizes in the regular weight variety, so long as you eat while hungry and don't starve yourself. However, if you're worried which you're losing too much weight, and then you definitely have several alternatives like

- Eat often, as a minimum three times within a day, which includes masses of protein, and lift weights to put on muscle.

- Eat a little more carbs (like fruits with low-glycemic) to place on a bit more fats.

- To summarize, there's normally no need to halt a keto weight loss plan to stop losing weight. This will manifest anyway, as you attain what your body perceives is the right weight for you.

The information supplied in this eBook will assist you right way to reach your success dream to lessen weight and hold suitable fitness for the duration of your lifestyles. Before you start every day, bear in mind and remind yourself about extraordinary advantages you reap while doing this food regimen and tell yourself that you could do this for enhancing your fitness and energy. Don't neglect to take measurements and pix earlier than you start your food plan, this is the great way to screen your progress and recollect this is not just for weight loss, this is for attaining better health throughout your lifestyles. Once again thank you for downloading our eBook and we hope you will achieve your dream weight and health.

About the Author

Hello! I'm Maria Phillips, passionate follower of ketogenic weight loss diet program. Ketogenic isn't always a weight reduction plan, it's far a life-style. I hate being obese and having a completely fatty body, we must be slimmer and active. While following this way of life, without understanding you are going to enhance your fitness and splendor with dramatic weight loss. I certainly recommend you to observe a ketogenic weight loss program and explore blessings your self.

How I feel

I feel great to be a ketogenic diet follower and one outstanding element is I pick and make my personal keto recipes with none deficiency of fats and protein. Due to busy work tensions, a variety of people won't capable of create or make very own recipes, so I need to help and share my recipes with the people who are looking for for right and healthy keto recipes.

-- [MARIA PHILLIPS]

Made in the USA
Middletown, DE
05 April 2018